Redneck Spirituality

—*Book One*—

Redneck Spirituality
Book One
Book Two
Book Three
Combined Edition
(Books 1 & 2)

&

The Courage of a Butterfly
An autobiographical novel
written under this author's full name,
Edmond E. Frank

Redneck Spirituality
—*Book One*—

Don't Paint

Your

Turds Pink

by
E. Egorhh Frank
"Coach Egorhh"

Copyright 2018
by Edmond E. Frank
All rights reserved.
No part of this book may be reproduced
by any means or in any form without
the express permission of the author.

ISBN 978-1-7327328-3-4

Dedication

For the one who has given my life—life!
He has taught me to live true to myself
in authenticity and honesty:
The two things that it takes for a man to know,
and to respect himself.

My journey has been one of magnificence and wonder
with him, an ever-present presence—
my silent invisible companion, dear friend, and mentor.

Glimpsing life through his perspective has been a privilege.
I dedicate this book to

The Angel

Epigraph

There are no coincidences.
Your life is run by your soul and everything
put before you is for your learning.

It is no mistake that something about this book
has attracted your attention.

Your soul knows there is something
for you here that you need.

Coach Egorhh

Table of Contents
Redneck Spirituality—Book One

Part 1—Life's Laws

PAGE

1	Life's Laws (listed)
5	Let's Talk About the Truth—
7	So What's This Writer's Agenda?
13	Take Your Time
15	Some Things You Need to Know
17	How Am I Doing?

Part 2—Reflections of Life

21	Peeling Onions
23	Omissions
25	Pity
26	One Single Lie
27	Actors in a Play
29	What Is
30	Destiny
31	Needs—Part One
33	Needs—Part Two
34	Needs—Part Three
36	A Cry in the Dark
37	Bug Brains
39	Playing It Safe
41	Reflections of Ourselves
43	A Good Day . . .
44	Thoughts Create
45	We Always Know
46	Integrity
47	All that I Am
49	About Changing
51	Think for Yourself

52	Faulting You
53	About Limitations
54	Fools
55	The Gift of Our Pain
56	In the Face of One's Pain
57	Selfish
59	What Is Right and Wrong
61	The Smallness of Our Mind
62	The Gift in Evil
63	Lessons
64	Death of a Different Sort
66	Into Her Care
68	Man's Greatest Danger
69	My Greatest Aspiration
70	The Sting of Truth
71	Always
72	On the Line
73	About Apologies
75	Anger
77	The Root Element of Wisdom
78	Being "Normal"
79	Perfect Perception
80	Count on Yourself
81	Weird
82	Change Your Mind—Change Your Life
83	Fearlessness of Innocence
84	Fear
85	Standing by Your Beliefs
86	Whole and Healed
88	Standards
90	Illusions of Security
92	Accept
94	Adults Do
96	Generations Past
98	Who You Really Are

99	Our Own Reality
100	Our World
101	About Blame
102	Being Who You Are
103	Right or Wrong
104	The Words We Use
106	Thoughts
108	Commitment
109	Death's Whisper
110	A Weapon of Fear
111	There in Balance
112	Its Lies
113	About Liars
114	Endless Possibilities
115	The Works of Others
117	No One's World is the Same
118	Taking Offense
119	Selfish Wants
120	Conventional Thinking
121	Wants and Demands
122	Maturity
123	Ticklish
124	The Blind Spot
125	Participation
127	To Be Cherished
128	Being Authentic
129	The Last Haunt
131	Epilogue

The Assessment

About the Author

Acknowledgments

The Las Vegas Creative Writing Critique Group:
Most were not in this venue, and some had resistance to the content herein. When you offer a perspective that is this different from the way most have been taught to see life—well, you just don't know where folks will take it. The critiques I received there were some of the most valuable.

The main reason most authors write is to touch the reader. The reader may choose to like what is written, or they may hate it. Either way, the writer has touched them and given them cause to think.

As an author, it is only those who don't give a shit who I've failed. So THANKS to you folks out in Summerlin for giving a shit—for allowing me to touch you, figuratively, of course.

The Sin City Critique Group:
Only a few were not of this venue (searching to understand and to make their lives better). Of those who were not, they were more loving and accepting—and open-minded.
They showed me where normal folks go when they aren't being led to stampede. And they helped me to write in ways to be better understood—and they did it with a sense of humor.

Their critiques were also very valuable, and mostly enjoyable. The times they weren't enjoyable was when I most needed to pay attention.

Thanks to my Beta Readers—too numerous to list here. I hope I added as much to your lives as you did mine.

To Bobby Daniels Graphics who did all the excellent work setting up the cover—a real artist.

And lastly, to my editors:

> **Toni Briegel**
> **Kitty Schuler**
> **Denise Sage**

Thank you all for the excellence of your advice.

Introduction

This book is about Spiritual Laws, the indelible truths of life—

WHOA!

Hey, just hold that thought. If you are like me, and someone comes along and tries to saddle me with some "law" or "truth" I might not agree with—well, that's about the time my pucker string gets *reee-aal* tight.

I get that—So feel free to call them *principals*, or *truisms*, whatever turns your crank. Thing is, like the physical *Law of Gravity*, they too *just are*. Ignore gravity and you are going to take a fall. Ignore these truths—these Spiritual Laws of Life—and no matter what you call them, your life will take the fall. The cuts and scrapes, the broken bones on which you hobble through life—those are called dysfunctions. Take a deep breath, loosen up that pucker string and go with it.

Now, just knowing something in your head, is like looking at it *out there*, and changes nothing. Knowing it in your heart is like looking at it *in here*—from the heart's perspective—a completely different life changing way of seeing it.

* * *

It's one thing to sit on the cliff over a deep sandstone canyon, and to look down at the Moki Indian dwellings tucked up under the overhanging wall. Seeing the tops of the cottonwood trees way down there in the bottom of that dry wash, you know that down there somewhere, there is water—and you're damned thirsty!

It's quite another thing to edge your way along the narrow ledges, the hot sun on your back making you shirt stick, and sweat trickle down into your butt-crack as you inch your way along with your ass hanging out over the abyss. It's a fear-filled journey to get to those dwellings under the over-hanging cliff and to stand in the doorways of what's left of those rock and mud homes.

You look down at the ancient finger prints still etched into that centuries dried mud. Then down at the sand and pebbles mixed with flint chips from the making of arrowheads and realize, you are standing on sacred ground.

You climb on down to the wash below using the foot and hand hollows cut centuries ago with stone tools, now allowing you to negotiate your way down that last near-vertical cliff.

Ah, but there is freedom in treading the ancient paths in the cool shade of those majestic cliffs with their black skirts of manganese stains—and then to drink cool sweet spring water from the same natural sandstone cistern where the long dead Moki once drank.

* * *

That, is what it is like to take that famous "eighteen-inch journey" between your head and your heart—to know something in your heart. It's not a mental thing—it's a scary, experiential/emotional/spiritual thing.

Section Two is about experiencing these Laws of Truth from the heart. Truths that also are ancient, long kept secrets hidden away by the leaders and preachers of our society—truths they replaced with lies to keep you enslaved to their own agendas. It is **NO** lie, that the truth will set you free.

In this book are listed the sixteen truths I think are the most important. There are many more, but these are a good beginning. These laws, if taken to heart and followed, will give you a new life, and freedom such that likely you can not now conceive. If by living these truths, a redneck like me can mend the broken bones of his own life's dysfunctions—so too, can you. Or perhaps you would rather wait to meet the Angel—we all do eventually. Y'know?

Surely you know that the Angel doesn't give many reprieves. But at a time when I was desperate to know the truth about life, he gave me the answers—and I discovered the courage to make that journey. I now pass on his truth to you. The courage you will need to find within yourselves. So from The Angel, to me, and now to you: *here's your reprieve. . . .*

I offer it to you—*without expectations.*

And that folks, that "without expectations" part, is the definition of a true gift. Accept this redneck's book—this gift—or don't. It's up to you.

You are the Creator of your life—

PART ONE

Life's Laws

The Truths of Life

NOTE:
You will likely want to refer back to this section occasionally. Consider placing a page marker on this page for easy referencing. Markers can be purchased at any stationary store—or just fold a piece of tape at the edge to make your own.

The Laws of Life

1—I am the Creator.

Most only take this to mean I create my own life. That is true. But to own it requires me to understand that there is nothing in my life that I have not had the deciding factor in creating. It is true, too, that all other Spiritual Laws presented here, are just aspects of this one. As you read through and comprehend the concepts in this book, you will get a sense of how this Law touches upon the infinite.

2—Thoughts create.

Look around you. Everything our species ever created began as a thought in someone's mind. As for the rest, there is an order to the universe. One that speaks to sentience—to feeling, sensing, understanding, creating—like us, but much more. It is a "Higher Power" infinitely beyond what our religions can conceive.

3—Thoughts are energy.

In being our own Creator, we choose in every second of life, the energy with which we are creating. It can only be one of two energies—the energy of *all that is love*, or the energy of *all* that is not love (fear).

4—The energy out, returns in kind

The energy of your every thought determines what comes to you in life—*love* or *fear*. This is that freedom of choice which is our greatest gift of all Creation. It is this choice which creates the path of our lives and the quality with which we walk.

5—The Universe always balances.

With every sorrowful thing, there is the potential for an equal joy, yet we are the creators in our lives. There is equal joy to be found in every sorrowful event, *If* we will look for, *and* accept it. The truth is, it is we who have chosen the sorrow, and it is we who must seek and choose the joy. The potential for both exists in balance within the universe, and we are but a shift of mind away, requiring no more struggle than the acceptance of our next breath.

6—The energy of thoughts must flow:

Once taken in, the energy of fear stays and is the initial cause of all sickness *if* it is not felt, acknowledged, and then released. Even love energy must be released—given back out—in order to flow.

7—Along with being the creator comes responsibility: one cannot BE the Creator and play the blame game.

One cannot, *not* create. Each person must accept responsibility for the totality of creating their life, especially for all thoughts and feeling associated in that process. *Blame is the abdication of responsibility, the greatest of all Mankind's dysfunctional lies.*

8—The world is not "out there"—it is "in here."

It is comprised of every thought, every belief, and every feeling you have. Your world is totally your responsibility because you are the only one who has the ability to respond—the ability to make it better or worse—loving or fearful. *Only you can change your mind.*

9—*Others are but a mirror for us to see ourselves.*

What we don't like in others is but the reflection of what we don't like in ourselves. If it were not also within us, we could never see it in them.

10—*The purpose of life is for those lessons.*

When we refuse the learning, the lessons will be presented again, more forcefully until we learn them—or die.

11—*Self-esteem requires integrity—it is the respect of your soul.*

What our heart feels, what we think, say, and do—all must align as the same, and be coupled with the strength of intension to be in integrity. Integrity commands esteem.

12—*Our lives are run primarily by our needs—then by our wants.*

As such, our lives are mostly run from an unconscious level. We all know what it is we want—few know what we need to have it. Needs are about the necessities—wants are about the quality.

13—*Our life is our sole possession—and so it is for everyone.*

We, being the Creator, have all the say in creating our own life—no say in the creation of anyone else's. They are always free to be, say, or do whatever they want—without actual harm to others.

14—Change is the constant of the universe.

Change is fearful. With everything we find fearful, change—the unknown—will be at its core. Fear? Fear is *not* a constant. It is a choice (Law 3). And sometimes, it is a barometer for change.

15—To create a functional life requires one to do one's own thinking.

The beliefs passed down through the generations, as well as by our religions, are generally accepted as truth. Even when those "truths" serve us falsely, few have the courage to think for themselves. It takes great courage to think differently in the face of family and/or religion. Dysfunction will always come when living the lies passed down to you by others.

16—Controlling anything outside ourselves is a fallacy.

We can only control another in as much as they will let us—or rather pretend to let us. And our world? See Law 8. Yes, we control our own world, because it lies within us.

Let's Talk About the Truth—

So these laws are the truths governing life—the ones some would call Spiritual Laws? But for many, "spiritual" is another way of saying "religious." This book is not about religion. That is not to say it does not recognize a "Higher Power."

Truth always uplifts. But lies—lies drive your life into the ground. The problem is, we have all been taught a boatload of lies—well meaning mostly—but lies. All have come from the people we trust the most. It is the same story for nearly everyone. Will you be one of the few to question, who will have the audacity to seek out the truth? Most won't. Most will accept those crash landings, and the resulting broken bones, and keep on hobbling through life on their dysfunctions—no courage in that, just painful ignorance.

For some, the mere sight of the ground rushing up to meet them, makes them reach out for the truth. For others, it is the crash, the burning chaos, and the ensuing ashes that sends them searching like a Phoenix for a way to rebuild their lives better.

For others like me, it is nothing less than the *Grim Reaper*, the *Angel of Death,* who forces us to look at our lies. By then it is usually too late. We generally go to our graves with a whimper or a wail, despising ourselves for never having the courage to search out the truth about life—especially, our own—and *accept* it.

Looking back, one can see so much clearer. When looking from a depth of six feet, that statement is no longer such a cliché'. Yet even then, very few reach out and grasp their courage, cover themselves with its mantle, and refuse the Angel. That is what it takes to *win* a reprieve—*and evolve.* Not many reach, not many cover, not many win.

And evolve? I have proposed it as in "accepting," and even "winning." Evolving in this life for you may be about "grasping"—*taking this reprieve*. If you wait for the Angel, it will likely be too late.

Melodramatic?—Maybe.

Still, no matter where you are in the order of all this, that you have this book in your hands says your soul believes there is something here you need. It is your soul that in every moment of life is providing you the lessons. These truths may not appear to be all that earth-shattering. Neither is the cocoon of a chrysalis—a soon-to-be butterfly. Make no mistake: These laws are a life-changing cocoon for you—the chrysalis—to evolve. And for the rest of your life, be a butterfly.

So What's This Author's Agenda?

Again, these Laws "just are." They don't need your approval—nor do I. My agenda here is merely to expose you to these truths.

Some will recognize their validity and accept them. They will change their minds *right now*, and, their lives—also, *right now*. Others won't. Still, exposing you to the truth will make you aware of the lies you never knew you believed—until *right now*. It may well take more pain and dysfunction in your life to convince you. That is your choice—again—*right now!*

"*Right now*"—do you wonder why I keep hammering on these two words? It is because as one who knows, *right now* is the only time there is—the only time you are guaranteed. Like I once did, *most folks waste it.*

Have you noticed how these laws are interwoven—like a cocoon? Just so, the concepts—beginning in Part Two—often involve aspects of more than one law. No need to memorize, it is only in knowing what they *mean* that you will know anything. The aim of the concepts is to show you that meaning—what life looks like in the reflection of the laws. If you don't understand something, the applicable laws are listed in an abbreviated form. Go back to the long explanations and re-read the laws as needed.

As a teen-ager, I once lived in a construction camp for a dam on the Acheloos River in Greece. My brother Mark and I often swam in that river, down in a gorge where the surface seemed to be almost still—although we knew there was a considerable volume of flow. Looking into the dark depths of the river there, that was clearly a given. My greatest wish for you is that the flow of this book will feel as deep to you now, as the Acheloos River felt to me then.

Some will plunge right into the cooling waters of this book. Some will not. Sharing these truths with someone searching, is helping. Saving is NOT my purpose. No one drowns in these waters. So, dabble your feet in the coolness of this river, or dive right in. Maybe you'd rather just stand on the bank and sweat. It's up to you

Every good book needs a hero. This time, that hero must be you. The simple truth is:

> *When you change your mind about anything,*
> *you change your whole life—forever!*

Frightening, isn't it? Do you see why I say **hero**? Yes, it does require courage. This is why so few people make the changes they say they want in their lives.

Again, to hammer it home one last time—my purpose here is to expose you to the truth. That you accept it and evolve—or not—is up to you. That part does not belong under any hammer in my hand. Many simply lack the courage. No matter how painful their life, they know it well. More comfortable is the pain of their known dysfunction, than the fear of an unknown change.

> *Are you one of the few with the courage to change*
> *and—like a butterfly—discover the beauty within yourself?*

My hammer is now in your own hand—the gift within this book. Every nail—every true belief—you choose to hammer home, will bring new joy into your life. Choose now to have the courage to change.

> *Can you not see that every caterpillar makes this same choice?*
> *And butterflies—do you think they ever have regrets?*

It is hard to be a fresh voice writing about Spiritual Laws and concepts that have been around all down through the ages. Even the ancient Greek philosopher, Socrates, talked about them.

***"The unexamined life is not worth living."*—Socrates**

Examining and understanding who you are, and what your true responsibilities are in life, is the crux of these Laws of Life.

Fresh? Different? What does this book have to offer that all those before it didn't? Perhaps it is the fact that in the past there have been few writers with the cajones to say it like it is—much easier, and profitable, to give you a feelie-good book to read. This is a workbook.

This is NOT a feelie-good workbook!

Can you ever have change by only looking at what feels good and supports you in your thinking? Your thinking creates your life—all, of it. If there is dysfunction in your life, it can only mean there is dysfunction in your thinking. Telling you things that feel good, only validates your thinking—the functional AND the dysfunctional, and changes nothing.

The things that can and do change your life, are those that *don't* feel good. These Spiritual Laws are the truth. If you are living a lie, seeing the truth will always be uncomfortable because it demands change. Change never feels good until after it becomes the known normal. Decide now if you want it. Again, living a dysfunctional life may not be all that enjoyable, but it does feel safer than making changes. Now, lets talk about the lies.

It is not "politically correct" to tell you just how badly your life has been "anal-lyzed." Shit! If you've even begun to accept these Laws of Truth, then you cannot help but begin seeing those dysfunctional lies—the ones you have been taught upon which you "should" base your life.

> *It might help to know that "should" is merely the shit from between someone's ears—usually not your own—and it stinks.*

If it stinks, why would we accept it? Face it—no one finds the smell of their own shit all that repulsive. Well, do you? If you did, it would make it difficult to live with yourself, wouldn't it? It's only other people's shit that we think stinks—no matter out of which end it comes.

Coming from one end you might pinch your nose and accept it. Coming from the other, not doing your own thinking is to pinch the nose of your mind. Their mental shit, then becomes your own, and you don't notice the stink.

Politics be damned! It also begs repeating—clearly—who those liars are that wiped all that "should" off onto your life. They are **your parents,** your *religions, the leaders of society—nearly all those whom you love or respect*. Why else would you accept those lies without question? Just know, it was never a deliberate thing. They too, pinched the nose of their mind—accepted it all before you—same as you. What if the person telling you all that "should" had been someone you didn't even know—some redneck, maybe like me?

Yes, puts it all in a different light—doesn't it? However, with me, you are free to think for yourself, and to question every word you read. Hell, I encourage you to question everything between these pages.

And the "should" between your own ears—is it your own? Does it uplift and nourish you with truth? The thing about shit is that it results from what has nourished you. What makes it stink so badly is when it comes from between someone else's ears, and has never nourished. Instead, it has made you a stinking victim in life.

Now to be honest, didn't I just tell you how *your life has been* "anal-lyzed"—how you have been a "stinking victim?"

> *Whoa, hey! Have I also been "should-ing" on you— or am I offering you a choice?*

The key words here are *"...your life **has been**"*—**PAST TENSE!**
Point is, that was the truth about your past. It is now up to you if that will be the truth in your future. Within the cocoon of these Spiritual Laws, that victimized pupa from your past now has a chance to become a butterfly.

Me? What do I get for rubbing all this truth in your face? I fully expect *some* will want to crucify me. Hell, Socrates was put to death for this same act of politically-incorrect-social-disobedience. My purpose in exposing you to these truths is simply to offer you an opportunity to make your world—and mine—a little better place.

I have no desire to be a preacher, or guru. I'm just tired of seeing this shit-storm of dysfunction swirling all around, and knowing the reasons behind it all—and yet not caring enough to open my mouth and risk condemnation. Twenty-five years ago, the Angel gave me a reprieve. This book and the one (or more) to follow, just may be his reason.

Take your time

This is not a big book, but if you're paying attention, it will be a long read. It is meant to be a workbook.

Some will read this book for the information---some will do the work. It all depends on if they came to this game to be a spectator in the bleachers, or as a player on the field of life.

Whether it is a hard copy or digital—doesn't matter. To work it, you will need a notebook, preferably one that is a ring binder—at some point you may need to add a page or three.

Currently this is Book One of Two—one binder will do. In the beginning, write only on the right side pages. The reason for this will be explained later. Write down the title and page number of the reflection, then answer the questions, do the exercises, and write down you own thoughts.

If you have no personal opinion—it's okay, you will soon. This is about self-discovery, and what you discover will be huge. Some will buy this book and read it for the information. They want knowledge—they don't want change.

The *bad* news first: *You will get change.*

The *good* news? Yes, you guessed it: *You will get change.* And, it will be the change you want.

And the *truth: There is no good or bad*—we'll discuss that later. For now, here is one clue. "Good and bad" reside only between your ears.

I guarantee that if you WORK this workbook, your life will be different—better. Maybe, you will make a difference for someone else, perhaps even one of those whom you love.

Without you, they may never have a clue about those lies. Pass this book on, or better yet, get another and pass that one on. The debt everyone owes to that Higher Power for the privilege of being alive *is to live a life that makes a difference.*

Could be that—like me—*now's your chance.*

Some Things You Need to Know

To this author, being a redneck means he has always lived life on the cusp of crudity. This book *says-it-like-it-is* with *in-your-face crudity*. This is the redneck way. Much of this material cries for just that approach. For the most part the language used will be as clearly written as this redneck can write it.

You have read the Laws—benign, do you think? Now it's time to look at what they mean in life. This is where things may start not-feeling-so-benign. **This** is where you will start seeing your viewpoint of life may not be the truth. **This** is where you will start seeing the lies you have been taught to believe.

Some of the following reflections will merely feel "off,"—is the writer redneck challenged? Maybe. *Some* will tweak your sense of propriety. *Some* you may feel are outrageously blasphemous.

Good!

As all speak to your own perceptions, these are the things that you need to look at—the ones that mean change for your life—if you accept them. Fact is, your soul sees the

truth in them, but your conscious mind sees only the change they require in your life, *and is afraid.* You now have only one of two ways to go:

Gather your courage and change. Or accept whatever dysfunctions you have going—and stop right here

The fact remains, you have already been exposed to the laws—to the truth. If the lies you've been taught are not yet apparent, they soon will be—right in your face. Your soul will see to it. Again, it is your soul that brought you to these pages. If any peace, love, or joy is missing for you—and you want it—then gather your courage *and keep on reading.*

Bottom line:
I may be the only person who has the right—even the obligation—to say this last thing to you. This is because,

I HAVE BEEN THERE . . .

When the Angel comes to take you home, he will either pick up a hero or a coward. That is the choice you have before you—

RIGHT NOW.

How am I Doing?

This is a workbook. When finished, likely you'll feel a need to know how you did. If you aren't interested in scoring yourself, then you've failed—failed to be honest.

Face it: This book would not be in your hands—or digitally in your face—if you did not want something from it. Here is what I am asking you to do. Make the following notations near the title of each reflection, either in your hardcover or notebook.

1. With every reflection presented, if you agree without resistance, just put a check mark.
These are things that were in your belief system to begin with.

2. If the reflection has pointed out something more—something new—then put a check with a plus sign.
(✓+)

3. If you feel anything negative, or even just an "off" feeling concerning it, then you have some resistance going on—it is a good thing when you think for yourself. Put a circle.
(O)

4. If you don't understand it—after having re-reading the applicable Laws listed—that is also considered resistance. Put a circle with a question mark beside it.
(O?)

5. If you understand, but don't agree, put an X beside your circle of resistance.
(OX)

6. And if it is something you don't agree with to the extent that you resent it, put an exclamation mark next to that X.
(OX!)

7. If at any time you find yourself in agreement with any showing a circle of resistance, simply add a check mark.
O✓—O?✓—OX✓—OX!✓

NOTE:
Please understand, these are reflections of the Laws of Truth. You may notice some may be very similar, just presented using different scenarios. That's right, they have been repeated. There is an explanation for this. Watch for it.

At the end of this book, you will find another explanation, this one on how to assess your progress through this book. Do NOT cheat yourself by flipping forward to read it before you have finished doing the work.

PART TWO

Reflections of Life

In the Light of the Laws

Peeling Onions

This book is about peeling an onion—the onion of your beliefs. In looking at the way you think about everything you will find that *who* you are is, *what* you believe. As previously mentioned, what you believe is often based on a whole lot of lies. This book is about looking at some of those lies and replacing them with truth. Indeed, you will find it is like peeling an onion: There will always be another layer underneath to peel—and often, there will be tears.

In general, the lies come from your society—other people wanting you to live your life to suit themselves, wanting to control, and essentially enslave you. You have been taught to see yourself as a victim with other people holding the power in your life—your government, your religion, your parents, your significant others, etc.

Understanding that you are the creator of your life, and that only you hold the responsibility—the ability-to-respond—is your first step. These spiritual laws I have offered you in this book are the truths.

Peeling your onion will be a journey—a wondrous journey you won't regret taking, regardless of the tears. And these truths are only the beginning. You will learn about many more—and will apply the nuances of them all in your life. There is great joy in living the truth and being the master of your life.

The responsibility of holding the reins of your life is a scary thing and requires more courage than most people have. Just remember to (1) *live your life in love and not fear.* You then (2) *need no courage,* because courage requires you to first have fear. (3) *One cannot love in the space of fear*—it is one of the laws. (4) *There can be no fear if you are loving.*

I've said it four times. I hope you have taken at least one to heart. *Living in love is what brings joy to life*—there, that's five. *Don't cha just love all this oowee-goowee?* Okay, six is enough.

——— – – – ———

See Life's Laws:
1   I am the creator.
2   Thoughts Create.
3   Thoughts are energy: Loving, or not loving (fear).
8   The world is not "out there"—it is "in here."
15   One must do one's own thinking.

Questions/exercises to consider:
- **This journey** is sometime called "The Hero's Journey." What do you think? *Write about it.*
- **Are you** seeing some of those lies yet? Do you feel the burn? *Again, write about it.*
- **Might you** actually be enslaved by the lies? Do you want to be free—or do you think all this is all a little bit "out there?" *Yup, write about it.*
- **Can you** afford the price of not looking at it?

Omissions

Just because someone is telling me the truth—just not the full truth—does not excuse them from being a liar anywhere except in their own twisted mind. If I accept another person's lie as my own truth without searching my soul—well, that just makes me lazy, and ignorant.

Regardless of my good intentions, your journey in life is your own. Don't just believe these thoughts of mine without first asking your heart. It is your heart that connects you to your soul.

I've told you nothing within this book that I don't believe to be true, and no lies of omission unless they be out of the ignorance of my own humanity—I'm searching, just like you. The fact you have this book in your hand confirms that about you. Again, my journey has lasted some 25 years. That is a lot of time to be searching one's own soul and one's world for the truth. If your search has just begun, I wish it to be as wondrous as mine has been.

See Life's Laws:
15   One must do one's own thinking.
7   Along with being the creator comes responsibility.
2   Thoughts create.
8   The world is not "out there." It is "in here."
10   The purpose of life is for those lessons.

Questions/exercises to consider:
- **Do you** ever tell incomplete truths—leaving out defining parts that would otherwise sway your meaning?
- **Those things** your parents, your religious leaders, and society told you were the truth—did you just accept them as being true? Most everyone in the world does. Y'know?
- **Do you** believe the lies now? List every lie you now see that you have believed.
- **Did you** have the courage?
  This question can only be answered in retrospect—AFTER you have finished this book. Your soul always
- knows the truth, both the truths about life, and the truths about *your* life. But few are willing to look inside. If you *work* this workbook, you will look—and you will write down what you see. Any lies you may find yourself living, will demand you change your thinking—and your life. ***This is the full truth of this book—nothing left out.*** Do you have the courage?
- Looking at life from the perspective of the Spiritual Laws, give understanding that cannot otherwise be seen. I will be offering that perspective in different scenarios as you progress through these pages. When you're done, I'm confident you will know exactly what the "full truth" means. Yes, the big question is one of courage. Just keep that in mind, for now. AGAIN, it can only be answered in looking back—after this workbook has been worked. Answer then: *Did you have the courage?*

Pity

What if pity were just the emotional reflection of a pious mind, and had nothing what-so-ever to do with compassion?

See Life's Laws:
8   The world is not "out there"—it is "in here."
3   Thoughts are energy: loving, or not loving (fear).

Questions/Exercises to Consider:
- **Yes, what** if? *Write about it.*
- **Oh, and** is there any room on your fridge door?

>>><<<

One Single Lie

There is more value in a single lie revealed, than in a hundred truths. That single lie tells you where *not* to place your trust. For those given to lying, it becomes a crap-shoot, with the odds at 100% that they *will* crap-out, and tell the whole world, *"I am someone you cannot trust!"*

Problem is, most in this world are busy looking at your integrity, while playing craps with their own. That's because any slips in yours is validating to their own dishonesty—thereby making it easier to live with themselves.

See Life's Laws:
11   Self-esteem requires integrity.
4   The energy out, returns in kind.

Questions/exercises to consider:
- **What about** you? Do you place more attention on the integrity of others, than on your own?
- **Once someone** has broken their integrity with you, can you ever trust them again?
- **What if** they were to admit the breach and try to clean up the mess? What then?
- **What about** your own messes? What messes have you neglected to clean up?

Actors in a Play

As a whole, humans spend most of their time engaged as actors in a play—usually a drama. We are taught from birth never to reveal our true feelings, our real selves. To do so, makes us vulnerable to those who would use such information to hurt us—especially, to hurt our feelings.

Truth is, I also played those fear based games of power, control, and manipulation. Once given the understanding of the Laws, I now choose love.

Given an understanding of integrity, I now choose friends who understand it also, and who can see it in me. Stepping off the stage—being exactly who I am—is the way to know my true friends, and them to know me.

And feelings?—I myself am the only one who holds the power over my pain. And too often, when seeing that someone I love—and thought I knew—is only an actor playing a part, I exercise that power.

——— — — — ———

See Life's Laws:
11   Self-esteem requires integrity.
7   Along with being the creator comes responsibility.

Questions/exercises to consider:
- **Can you** see that what we are discussing here is your façade—the pink paint?
- **Do you** see that until you step off that stage, anyone who loves you, is really just loving your facade—not the real you? Is there a real you hiding behind a facade.
- **The lie** is that your facade protects you from the judgments of society. But you know your facade doesn't protect you from anything except your own feelings—don't you?
- **What don't** you think is acceptable about you?
- **What change** to your thinking will it take to muck the horse shit out of that stall?
- **Can anyone** wearing a facade ever be in integrity?

What Is

With those I would want to hold in close, it is not about accepting them. That's a given with everyone I know. It is merely about what is—about what is their integrity. In my experience of them, are they someone I would give my trust?

Given my experience of what they say they want, and the things they do—is it the same? Do their intentions match their results, *and do they seem happy with it all?*

See Life's Laws:
11   Self-esteem requires integrity.

Questions/exercises to consider:
- ➢ **What** besides integrity do you require to allow someone into your inner circle?
- ➢ **Do you** recognize the integrity in others?
- ➢ **Did Law** 11 give you needed insight to do so?
- ➢ **If they** aren't ". . . happy with it all," could it be that theirs is a pretense of who they think they must be, for your approval—but aren't?

Destiny

The fact that I'm still alive, means I have a destiny. I've not yet finished what I'm here to do—or learned what I'm here to learn. *AND,* I haven't yet given up the struggle.

But then hey, who says life need always be a struggle? Some things I've learned along the way have been absolutely inspiring!

See Life's Law:
10   The purpose of life is for those lessons.

Questions/exercises to consider:
- **Do you** believe that in the pre-existence, we set goals up for ourselves to accomplish in life?
- **What goals** do you think you might have set? Which ones are yet to be accomplished?
- **Do you** believe that when we lose that innate drive to accomplish things, we soon die?
- **Is your** life a struggle, or a wondrous journey? Write about it.

Needs—Part One

My physical needs are those things I must have in order to sustain me in life. Funny thing is, my soul's needs are always about experiencing and knowing *who I am.* I have no soul needs that depend upon *others* to get filled. Oh, other people can, will, and do, help me in seeing what I need to see about me. *But that is never dependent upon them changing or doing anything other than being who they are.*

Experiencing life and coming to know myself—those are the things my soul needs. Beyond my physical and soul needs all else I may hunger for are just wants—like candy—they are not needed to sustain my life or my soul. Still, getting to that place of knowing myself completely, is always a work in progress, and the true work that I—and everyone else—am here in life to do. The more work we get done, the sweeter the candy.

See Life's Laws:
12   Our lives are run first by our needs—then our wants.
10   The purpose of life is for those lessons.
1   I am the creator.
9   Others are but a mirror for us to see ourselves.

Questions/exercises to consider:
- **List some** physical things you need for the survival of your body.
- **List some** spiritual/soul things you need for the survival of your soul/spirit.
- **Now take** a magic marker and mark those things that require something of others that you currently are not getting.
- **Write about** how your un-acceptance of them is what holds you hostage and makes you forever unfulfilled?
- **What do** you need to change in your thinking to make them acceptable?
- **Do this** exercise: Take both your index fingers and point then inward at yourself. Now say: "The correction *always* goes here."

Needs—Part Two

Consider: We all need love. But love is something I need to be able to give myself before ever having the ability to give it to someone else. Once I accept myself and discover self-love, only then can I see my true need is to give my love to others. But receiving love from others? That is merely a want, the candy the Law will provide.

Whatever we want to get, must first be given—and, we must first have it to give it. To have love we must first love ourselves. The energy of love begins within you—and for you.

See Life's Laws:
6   The energy of thoughts must flow.
4   The energy out, returns in kind.

Questions/exercises:
- **Real love** has no expectations—does yours? Write about it . . .
- **This is** a difficult concept for many to understand. Did I need to repeat it for your understanding?
- **Has someone** ever shown you love completely unexpectedly—and without expectations? Write about it.
- **Is it** possible that under the Laws of Life, this was your love being returned? Again, write . . .

Needs—Part Three

The very act of giving love to others guarantees receiving love back. It does not guarantee receiving it from those to whom it was given. When you have love for yourself, that will never be the issue. Real love is a gift. And real gifts never carry expectations.

My wife loved me the best she could—but her love carried expectations. My love too, had its own expectations back then—the expectation of it being returned in the same manner given. I still love her—always will—but without expectations. We are no longer together—for me, she was the price of learning real love.

My love for her will always survive. It has its payback in the giving. But for a relationship to survive, love must be returned. If it is not, then the relationship is only about one—or both—person's fear-filled needs.

With us, it was both. We gave one another the lessons and I learned. Did she?—I don't know. What we get from others is limited by what we are capable of receiving. I do know that I will always be grateful for what I received from her.

Very few people know what real love means. From my experience of her—now, I do. It was a true gift she gave me—though at the time, it didn't feel like it. Still, I know that the next woman I love will be loved without expectations—will her love be the same. If she lives by the Spiritual Laws, it is a sure thing.

―――― – – – ――――

See Life's Laws:
4 The energy out, returns in kind.
13 Our own life is our sole possession. Just so, it is for everyone.

Questions/exercises:
- ➢ **Have you** ever had a failed love relationship?
- ➢ **Did it** end with hard feelings on someone's part?
- ➢ **If so,** can you see how that person's *love* was only a fear-filled need?
- ➢ **Was that** person you?—Yep, write about it—all of it.

A Cry in the Dark

"If it's not love, it is a cry for love." Ah, so very true a statement!

What can also be said is this: Such cries are always made in the vast darkness of fear—a place that is only dark because the ones crying, refuse to turn on the light switch and face the truth about themselves

---

See Life's Laws:
8   The world is not "out there"—it is "in here."
7   Along with being the creator comes responsibility.

Questions/Exercises:
- **Do you** think that those who are crying for love regard themselves as a victims in life?
- **Do you** cry for love? Or do you just give love?
- **Is it** possible that those unwilling to give love, are most likely to be the ones crying for love?
- **Face it**—we have all cried for love—most do it on a regular basis. Question is: are you going to flip that light switch? *Write about the truth it would reveal.*

Bug Brains

There's life in the ride, in the cooling of sweat or freezing of nosehairs in the wind. There's life in the bug brains on our teeth. And especially, there's life in keeping our own brains off the bumper of the next drunk we pass.

Ah yes, the *experiential* stuff of life—

There is *experiential* stuff and there is *spectator* stuff. Do spectators really live life, or does truly living require having the courage to follow one's joy regardless of the price? Are we accepting the experience of whatever comes? Most of all, do we have the courage to move past our fears?

To accept the pleasure means being willing to accept the pain, equally. The universe always balances. Yes, life is about all of that. But beyond it all: The choice is bug brains on our teeth—or just in our mind's eye.

Yes, the choice is to ride, or not to ride—truly ride.

See Life's Laws:
14   Change is the constant of the Universe.
11   Self-esteem requires integrity.

Questions/exercises:
- **Make a** list of your favorite things you like to do in your life, which are experiential? Which are spectator things?
- **What spectator** things do you want to make experiential?
- **What things** do you want to do, but don't because they are too dangerous or expensive?
- **What do** you need to do to change that?
- **Will you?**

Playing It Safe

Playing life safe is the same as playing to die. To not do what one loves because it involves an element of danger is to not live.

For me the real danger was never about something so simple as the possibility of death—rather it was in the certainty of the price I would pay if I did not allow a loved one to run my life.

Sadly, avoiding danger is what is *normal* for most in this life. Does this mean that most in the world are just standing in line waiting to die? Seems so . . .

For me back then, it was so—but then I paid the price. The loved one is no longer in my life. And I no longer stand in that line with all those *normal* folks.

So, do you consider yourself to be *normal?* Because if you do, well maybe it is time for you to step out of line—to truly live—to be the master of your own life. Maybe you are about to become *not normal*—like me. And yes—you will pay a price. Whatever it is, it will be worth it.

There is no safety in my life—never was. But there is self-respect—and there is joy in doing what I love.

See Life's Laws:
13   Our own life is our sole possession. Just so, it is for everyone.
11   Self-esteem requires integrity.
3   Thoughts are energy: Loving, or not loving (fear).
4   The energy out, returns in kind.

Questions/exercises:
- **Make a list** of the things you would love to do, but don't because it is not safe.
- **Which ones** are not safe because they are not acceptable to someone you love?
- **Which one** will you choose to do first?

Reflections of Ourselves

What I see in others is but a reflection of myself. That is the Spiritual Law.

Where it involves family, most choose to view our very worst, then blame our parents and see it only as a reflection of them. What if we were to apply the Law, only choose a better reflection?

> To hear our own wisdom in the voice of a grandfather
> Feel our nurturing heart through that of a grandmother
> Know the ferocity of the love in a mother's. protective arms
> Experience the support in a father's work-hardened hands

No, most don't look to the joy to be found in the reflection of our parents. Perhaps it is just as well. For in our pain, we find our greatest lessons. That is what pain is for.

The pain and sorrow—or the joy: One extremes comes from fear—the other, from love. The combination of it all, is what makes us human. It defines the breadth of our existence, here, in this life.

See Life's Laws:
3   Thoughts are energy: Loving, or not loving (fear).
9   Others are but a mirror for us to see ourselves.
7   Along with being the creator comes responsibility.

Questions/Exercises:
- **What Positive** aspects of you do you consider as being a reflection of your parents? List them.
- **What negative** aspects of them, do you refuse to reflect in you?
- **What negative** aspects do you wish were not reflected by you?
- **At some** time in the future—after you have finished both of these workbooks—come back and answer this last question again? *Then write about it all.*

A Good Day...

Did I have a good day? You bet! All my days are good days.

What do I mean? Pretty simple: It's a choice. And the alternatives—bad day or no day—really suck!

And, what about a "just okay day" you ask? Look at it this way: Is having a "just okay" life any different than having "no" life?

See Life's Laws:

3   Thoughts are energy: loving, or not loving (fear).
8   The world is not "out there"—it is "in here."

Questions/Exercises:
- **What kind** of day are you having today?
- **If it is** anything less than a good day, will you choose better tomorrow?
- **How** about choosing to have a *great* day every day? Write about it.

Thoughts Create

Truth is, your whole life is just the expression of how you look at it. Summed up, it is your thoughts expressed.

See Life's Laws:

8   The world is not "out there"—it is "in here."
2   Thoughts create.
3   Thoughts are energy: Loving, or not loving (fear).

Questions/Exercises:

> **Do you** want to see your life from a different perspective? If no—Why not?
> **Is it** possible that because you are here reading this, the true answer is *yes?* Again—why?
> **Do you** know that not one person has ever read a self help book while thinking his/her life was perfect?

We Always Know

How could I lose my self-esteem? Simple: by living outside of my integrity—by not being the same on the inside, as on the outside—by saying or doing other than I really am.

In the higher mind of my soul, I will always know. Soul uses the truth of integrity as the yardstick by which it measures and meters out self-esteem.

I can sometimes con my conscious mind into believing a lot of illogical shit. It has a huge stake in seeing me as being *in the right*—one that sometimes stretches the limits of sanity. But I can't bull-shit my soul. It runs on truth—and nothing but the truth. Y'know?

See Life's Law:
11   Self-esteem requires integrity.

Questions/Exercises:
- **Does your** soul need a baseball bat bigger than *integrity* to tell you what you must do?
- **There are** very few people who aren't holding a big load of shit concerning the relationship between their integrity and their self-esteem. By withholding that self-esteem their soul will rub that shit in their face. How badly does it make your life stink? *Take this one seriously and write about it.*

Integrity

Honor is not about the integrity *others* see in *me*—it's about the integrity *I* see in *me*. Integrity means that what my heart says, what I say, and what I do, are all the same and held together with true intention.

Integrity is a gift given to me, that only I can give. When I am in integrity, I honor me. There is a certain integral strength in me such that I need have no heroes *out there,* for I am a hero *in here.* This is what I know. This is what others see, and it matters not if they honor it—at least not to me.

> *And yet honor me they will—both in respect and trust.*

See Life's Laws:
11   Self-esteem requires integrity.
13   Our own life is our sole possession. Just so, it is for everyone.

Questions/Exercises:
- **Did you** understand the concept —*We Always Know*—the one offered prior to this one?
- **If not,** do you understand it better now? How so?

All that I Am

Like I once did, most folks need to tell themselves a lie or two every time they wake up, just to get themselves through the day. If they didn't—if they faced the truth—they'd have to change. And their whole life would change.

But what is the cost of not facing the truth? That cost is the price most are willing to sell their souls for, rather than to pay.

By not being honest with myself—not following my heart—I was simply lying to my soul. The extreme penalty your soul will eventually extract for lying, is your life—cancer, stroke, heart disease—you get it . . .

For me, it was a blood clot on the lung. But then, that part is immaterial, as is my lie.

What is important, is that when faced with the undeniable presence of the Angel of Death, I got real honest, real fast—and survived. Thing is, had someone explained all this to me before, would I have merely questioned his or her sanity? Would I have still denied my lies?

See Life's Laws:
2   Thoughts create.
14   Change is the constant of the Universe.
6   The energy of thoughts must flow.

Questions/Exercises:
- **Are you** questioning my sanity now?
- **Consciously** or unconsciously, *if* there something you need lie about to your self, or a loved one—maybe even to the world—you know it. **Is there?**
- **If there** is, here are your only choices:
  1. Live your short but comfortably dishonest life.
  2. Or have the respect of your eternal soul—
- *Choose.*

About Changing

When the bullets are flying and bombs exploding—facing those things with courage is what most equate with heroism.

Then there are other things—like things that come so easily and naturally to a caterpillar, but require a very special kind of courage from us. Looking at what lies within and making changes is also what heroes are about.

Facing death and the unknown beyond—is there a comparison to facing life, and changing? Who you become when you change your mind, and who you become when dead to this particular lifetime, are equally irreversible. You can never go back to who you were.

See Life's Laws:
14   Change is the constant of the Universe.
8   The world is not "out there"—it is "in here."
15   To create a functional life requires us to do our own thinking.

Questions/Exercises:
- **Change is** such a simple thing. Why do you think it promotes such fear?
- **What is** it about your own life, that you want to change? *Make a list.*
- **What change** to your thinking would be required? Make a list for each one—remember, this change cannot require anyone else to change their own thinking, or their lives, in any way.
- **In light** of *The Laws of Life* do you get that making this change to your thinking is the critical first step—that all other steps will follow without effort or conscious thought.

Think for Yourself

What I might feast on as a delicacy, another might find repugnant in the extreme, usually because someone once told them it was. It's not about what tastes good, nurtures or gives growth, rather it's about prejudice.

So it always is when we don't think for ourselves. Is it any wonder humanity is so slow to change—and to grow?

We are so attached to our children seeing everything the same way we do. Like mules pulling the family cart we pass down the same blinders we have always worn. They put them on, same as we once did—trusting us—without a thought.

―――― ― ― ― ――――

See Life's Law:
15   To create a functional life requires us to do our own thinking.

Questions/Exercises:
- ➢ **There you** have it—the same concept presented in two different ways. Did one grab you more than the other? Why?
- ➢ **Can you** see how perception is a choice?
- ➢ **How much** of your perception is taken from the beliefs of others?
- ➢ **What might** you be missing by not thinking for yourself?
- ➢ **Now's the** time to refer to your list from the previous reflection. Did you change your thinking about anything? Do you think your family still sees you the same?
- ➢ **Is your** child wearing your blinders? *Write about that.*

Faulting You

How can I fault you for having the same weaknesses as I? Listen-up and know: I will deal with my weaknesses. Yours are not my rightful concern.

And, I thank you for pointing out something in me, I needed to see.

See Life's Laws:

9   Others are but a mirror for us to see ourselves.

13   Our own life is our sole possession. Just so, it is for everyone.

Questions/Exercises:
- **What bothers** you most about the people closest to you? *Make a list.*
- **Now with** each thing ask yourself: "Could I ever see this in you, were it not also in me?"
- **Now ask** yourself this: "How can I place blame without taking responsibility?"
- **That** *is* what most folks do. Does it work? Do you want to continue doing it? *Write about it.*

About Limitations

We all choose our limitations. They are our security from having to be more than we think we are.

See Life's Law:
8	The world is not "out there"—it is "in here."

Questions/Exercises:
- **What would** your life look like if there were no limitations?
- **How many** of your limitations consist of those lies others have told you about life?
- **Are any** of them lies you have accepted, and now tell to yourself?
- **Have you** passed them on to your own children?
- **Did you** notice how this concept is like a twin to (Think For Yourself)?
- **If you** haven't already, write about all the shit from your own life that you have rubbed onto your child's.
- **Can you** smell it now?

Fools

If I think I'm a fool: *I am*—but only for thinking so poorly of myself. What other people think is really none of my business. What I know, is that making it my business demands a facade.

Maybe a fool is someone who wants to know others but is too cowardly to expose his or her true self. The facade they show, only speaks of the cowardly fool that they have become.

Only a fool would lie about who they are, then expect that when others like them, it is the truth.

See Life's Laws:
2   Thoughts create.
8   The world is not "out there"—it is "in here."

Questions/Exercises:
- **Do you** show a facade to other people—it's something we've all been taught to do. Y'know?
- **If so,** how does it serve you, or does the fact you think you need it, make you a cowardly fool?—**Ouch!**
- **Do you** see, that all that pink paint does, is erase your real self from this world? *Write about this.*
- **Fools**—been beating the shit out of that term. Do you see how this whole facade thing we've all been taught to do, is just fucking foolish? *Write down your thoughts.*

The Gift of Our Pain

If it is in my life, it is my creation. All emotional pain is created in my own mind, and always when it is dwelling on my past. Whether five seconds or five years, the event has already happened. How can it be my own creation, you ask? Why would I create such pain?

The gift of my pain is in the lesson, the "miss-take." It enables me to remember not to create the same "miss-take" again. We are simply built to succeed. We cannot succeed when we are unwilling to own our pain. We cannot succeed if we blame.

See Life's Laws:

7   Being the creator requires responsibility.
8   The world is not "out there"—it is "in here."
10 The purpose of life is for those lessons.

Questions/Exercises:
- **List some** of the more painful things you have going in your life.
- **For each** thing list the person or persons who are to blame.
- **Now consider** Law 1—yes, look it up.
- **Can you** see how it is indeed, all in your own mind?
- **Now ask** yourself this question: How fucked-up am I?
- **If you** had an answer for the above question, do you realize your "miss-take" yet? Go back two reflections to "Fools" and re-read the first sentence.

In the Face of One's Pain

Some choose to spend their lives mourning for the loss of a loved one—and many view it as a loving thing. The truth is: mourning is not about love—and for most; it is a natural and healthy thing.

It is about us dealing with, and moving past our pain in the fact our life no longer includes them. Yet for some, it becomes about us using that loved one's death as a inviolable reason for not having the courage to live life as it now is.

How does one talk honestly about such an unflattering thing as cowardice in the face of one's pain? Is it so much different than cowardice in the face of one's fear? Or is it the same?

See Life's Laws:
8   The world is not "out there"—it is "in here."
14   Change is the constant of the Universe.

Questions/Exercises:
- **Are there** any fears in your life that you are unwilling to face?
- **Is there** any pain that you are unwilling to face?
- **Do you** know that a coward is one who won't deal with their fears or their pain?
- **Is this** you? If so, is this who you want to be?

Selfish

Are we being selfish, those of us who live our lives to suit our own wants and needs? Or is it really those who expect us to live our lives to suit theirs, who are the selfish ones?

So call me selfish. To find someone who lives their "selfish" life the same way I do mine, would be to treasure every moment spent *being selfish* together.

We only have this life, and the time right now, to live it. It is all we are given. Why would others expect us to give it away—and even admire us for not living our life to its fullest?

To put your life on the line—being willing to fight against those who would try to enslave you and your loved ones—yes, that is courageous. And I've got to admit: I'm proud to have done that.

Jesus died, martyred on a cross, and many see that as a holy act, and sacred. I would never denigrate their beliefs. But for the rest of us, we are NOT Jesus. When there is no war—no one trying to enslave or kill our loved ones—it is just not the same sacred act, to be a martyr, giving our life for others.\

Have you ever noticed how these "martyrs" take delight in climbing up on a cross, then reminding everyone of their sacrifice? Why is it so hard to see that they are really only a coward in disguise—someone who has not the courage to live their own life? They are only on that cross because from there they get to abstain from living life, and blame it on you. And too, from there they get to look down on you?

See Life's Laws:
13   Our own life is our sole possession. Just so, it is for everyone.
1   I am the creator.

Questions/Exercises:
- ➤ **Are you** seeing how the rules of society have twisted the concept of selfish into one of its greatest lies? Write about it.
- ➤ **Do you** see it as a lie to admire sacrifice as a loving unselfish act, when at the time, there was no actual threat present?

What Is Right and Wrong

Right and wrong are not all inclusive: What is "right" and what is "wrong" is only so in my own mind. *I* don't have the *right* to expect that others think as *I do.*

Next time you are tempted to say "Oh, that is just *so* wrong . . ." consider changing that by adding "Oh, *in my mind*, that is just *so* wrong . . ."

Then—if you want to evolve—you might let go of all you consider *wrong,* and just talk about the *right.* "Oh yeah! I think that is *so* right—

And then, you might even evolve so far as to let go of *right and wrong* entirely! And just look at what is *loving—or not so loving.* That will cause you to look at yourself, and who you are.

Right and wrong are your judgments of what others are doing. *But loving or not . . .Now that, requires you to look at you and who you are being.*

Your life is really all about you—who you are being right now, and who you want to become. And that, is always about being loving—or not.

See Life's Law:
3   Thoughts are energy: loving, or not loving (fear).

Questions/Exercises:
- **Everyone** has been taught what is right or wrong. Do you think it is the same for everyone?
- **Do you** think your rights and wrongs are solely dependent on who your teacher was?
- **Can you** see that loving is about your feelings—your energy—and not your judgments?
- **Loving or** not—what is your own choice about it? Write down your thoughts.

The Smallness of Our Mind

So often we men, equate sexual conquest with manliness. Why is this so? Isn't it true, it is the woman who *lets us?* She isn't conquered, she doesn't surrender—she *accepts.* Anything else would be rape.

Another equally macho fallacy, also requiring another to *"let us,"* is that if we can make another appear as *less than*, then we appear as *more than*.

In both cases, we are only displaying the smallness of our mind—and sometimes, our member.

See Life's Law:
16   We only control ourselves.

Questions/Exercises:
- **Come on** guys, you do know the truth—both of them—now, don't you? *What do you think?*
- **But hey**—after a lady sees your small mind do you really believe you can ever be a conquistador with your member?
- **Does sex** have to be a conquest with you? Do your dealings with other men require a put-down? Are you willing to open your little **macho** mind? *Yes, write about it.*
- **And maybe** this is no reflection on you. Still it does reflect one of society's lies. Which one?—*Write.*
- **This one** is about the guys—and that doesn't mean you ladies can't express your thoughts—

The Gift in Evil

Is it possible that the "good" in good, is really the gift in evil? How else can one savor all that is good in life, without having known that which is not?

See Life's Laws:
9   Others are but a mirror for us to see ourselves.
3   Thoughts are energy: loving, or not loving (fear).
4   The energy out, returns in kind.
5   The Universe Always Balances.

Questions/Exercises:
- **Do you** see that we humans always need something to match things against, in order to consider their magnitude?
- **Do you** think it is the same with God—or whatever that higher power is, in which you may believe?
- **If your** higher power is only the good, how does "he/she/it" know anything about bad—or how bad you might be?
- **Does a** fish know air if it has only experienced water? *Write down your thoughts.*

Lessons

Our higher self—that part of all humanity which is of God—knows: The experiences in life we need for our growth, will always be presented to us repeatedly until we open ourselves to the lessons. It is of those reoccurring happenings in our lives, that we need to be especially aware. When we don't accept the lessons, they will only show up again more forcefully—more painfully—the next time.

And the lesson beyond the lessons? It is not God who bites us on the ass—it is our unwillingness to accept the lesson, and the gift it offers to our growth. The lesson beyond the lesson is one of appreciation.

See Life's Law:
10   The purpose of life is for those lessons.

Questions/Exercises to Consider:
- **Have you** been bitten on the ass lately?—You can bet you have.
- **If you** don't think so, then your life must be completely peaceful. Is it?

Death of a Different Sort

I think dying is just a freeing—a change in consciousness to the soul's greater awareness, and a leaving behind of one's physical body when it can no longer serve that soul. This is a standard belief.

Yet there are other deaths in life. There is the death one experiences when one leaves behind a limiting belief—is freed from the encumbrances of that belief—replacing it with one that serves. In the greater truth of that new consciousness, has the old you not died, and been left behind?

As with all death, here too is permanence: *Again, you can never go back to the life you knew.*

See Life's Laws:
8   The world is not "out there"—it is "in here."
2   Thoughts create.

Questions/Exercise:
- **Are you** only this physical body? Or is that just the vehicle for this mind and for its every thought, every belief, every perception that you hold about yourself and your world
- **Can you** see that when you change any belief, you change the "who" you were and become someone else?
- **If it** happens that the belief you change was not one of truth, but one that limited you, can you see that you have now evolved—that the person you have become is now *more than* the person you were?
- **Would you** mourn for that the person you were—who's now dead, never to return? Or would you rejoice for the person you have become?
- **All of** the above questions could be answered with a *yes* or *no*. Do you think the above concept represents thinking that is beyond the norm? Do you think it deserves answers beyond yes and no? There are many such concepts in this book just as deserving. If you have not given them that respect, go back now and do so. This is your workbook, to work—or not. The respect is also yours, given to yourself by working this workbook—or not.

Into Her Care

A birth is a gift to a mother by the Creator—a soul given into her care and nurturing from the moment of conception. Her pain on birth is merely an indication, a reminder from her Creator of its worth. This sense of worth is a gift she may—or may not—pass on to the world with her loving responsible care, teaching her child the ways of life.

The joys of her work—and its awesome responsibility—sometimes she shares with her man. Together, they leave the world a legacy. Sometimes that works out for the best—sometimes for the worst. And sometimes it is the worst that makes it work out for the best.

How I would live my life, is how you must live yours. You must be the next me.

Like a job description for most parents, this is the belief each tries to instill into their child. Many parents stay on the job long after the child is an adult. Everyone has this same personal need to leave something of themselves in this world. Selfish or not—this is the standard mantra of parents from time eternal.

Will we teach our children to be our best self, or worst? With most parents, it is both. Consciously, it doesn't much matter until comes the time for dying—and for that child to carry on.

The questions then, to ask of their child are serious. Just how much did you grow in this life? Did I give you the same legacy as was given me? Or did I give you one better? And perhaps by my poor example, I only gave you *the chance,* to be more?

Ultimately, your children create their own lives, and by the way they learned to perceive life from you, whether that is truth—or lies. More than anything, I write this book for my own child, just to give him the chance by knowing that—from my sometimes poor example—*he can do his life better.*

---— — — ---

See Life's Law:
1   I am the creator.
2   Thoughts create.
13 Our own life is our sole possession. Just so, it is for everyone.
15 To create a functional life requires us to do our own thinking.

Questions/Exercises:
- **Given the** above questions, what legacy were you given?
  I can guarantee from experience that death always poses the important questions. How do you think your children would answer? Would you be okay were your child to become *more* than you?
- **Could it** be that by seeing and doing life differently, they have become more—and it is you who cannot see it?
- **Do you** approve of who your child is?
- **If you** didn't teach them by the time they're eight, it's probably too late.
- **Teach them** WHAT, you ask? Try, just living in the space of love.

Man's Greatest Danger

As a species, any animal we choose to view as a threat, we will always attack. Steeped in the energy of fear, we seek to kill it first. The truth is, it is always in that endeavor wherein lies the greatest danger. For this is our *normal* response to *everything* we perceive as a threat—*including someone who merely thinks differently.*

See Life's Laws:
16   We only control ourselves.
13   Our own life is our sole possession. Just so, it is for everyone.

Questions/Exercises:
- **Are you** a "normal" person?
- **Do you** often rail at and demand other people see things the same way you do?
- **What are** those things? Religion? Politics? Sex?—Or something equally irrelevant to your well-being?

My Greatest Aspiration

To know the depths of the love
my heart can hold.
To fly the rarified skies
where resides my soul.
To kindle the embers
for others with compassion.
To burn with the life fulfilling
fires of my passions.
To have the courage to abide
without fight or flight
where only love resides.

See Life's Laws:
3   Thoughts are energy: loving, or not loving (fear).
8   The world is not "out there"—it is "in here."

Questions/Exercises:
- **What are** your own aspirations?
- **What haven't** you done that you want to do?
- **Are you** being exactly who you want to be?
- **Have you** any dreams that have yet to come true?—List them all.

The Sting of Truth

People will always talk. But when I get angry with what they say about me, that is when I need most to remember: The angrier I am, the more their words have carried the sting of truth.

See Life's Law:
9   Others are but a mirror for us to see ourselves.

Questions/Exercise:
- **Have you** felt that sting lately?
- Is it possible that it is your soul, giving you this same lesson, once again?
- **Whoa!** Did that one also sting?
- **Did it** sting worse this time, than the last?
- **How many** more stings will it take before you die of anaphylactic shock?

Always

Yes, sometimes in life you must face death in order to truly live.

But always! —Always, you must face your fears, if you want to live with respect—your own respect!

You can live as long as you need to, without the respect of others. You cannot live long without your own. Your own respect is the response of your soul.

See Life's Law:
10   The purpose of life is for those lessons.

Questions/Exercises:
- **Are there** any fears that you keep silent and secret, and refuse to face?
- **Is one** of those secret fears that others will also see you as a coward? Been there—done that too.
- **Does your** body have the ability to repair injuries and/or cure diseases?
- **What is** it do you think, that commands your body's abilities?
- **Yes, to** cure or not to cure? Is that not the question?—the one always at your soul's discretion.

On the Line

Time? Money? Such excuses are like farts in a hurricane when it is my life on the line. Funny thing is, when it comes to being someone I can respect—my life is *always* on the line!

See Life's Law:
11   Self-esteem requires integrity.

Questions/Exercises:
- **Would you** rather die making excuses—farting into a hurricane—instead of doing the work of becoming someone you respect? *That is the work this book asks you to do.*
- **Will dying** without self-respect ever be okay with you? Been there—done that too. Wasn't okay with me. *Don't cheat yourself—write down your thoughts.*

About Apologies

I try to live life in the space of love—never—intending harm to anyone. This does not guarantee that others won't be harmed, or at least feel they have been. Either way, I never apologize. Rather, I acknowledge their feelings, and acknowledge my "miss-takes," in those times when I would do something differently, if faced with that situation again.

Living life in the space of love is the highest and best anyone can do, and requires no apology—ever.

Physical pain—intended or unintended—is physical, and I might unintentionally bear responsibility for its cause. But mental pain? My feelings are always my own choice and responsibility. Apologies from another only offer an opportunity for me to shirk that responsibility—which would deny me the ability to respond to my pain.

Hanging the responsibility for my feelings on another, guarantees I will carry that pain indefinitely. *Taking responsibility for someone else's choice of feelings is what an apology actually is. As such, it is one of the most insidious of lies anyone can tell.*

See Life's Laws:
1   I am the creator.
7   Being the creator requires responsibility.
8   The world is not "out there"—it is "in here."

Questions/Exercises:
- ➤ The next time you think you need to apologize to someone, ask yourself, "Did I do actual physical harm to them?" If it is mental pain, then for you to take credit for it, is to say, "Sure, I know you choose your own feelings, but I don't hold you capable of dealing with them—here, let me save you." Write about anything you think might validate such a statement.
- ➤ Confused? Go to Section One and re-read the three laws listed above in their entirety. You are now privy to one of society's greatest lies. How do you feel about this?
- ➤ It's true that not apologizing—not telling society's most acceptable lie—will probably lose them as your friend. The real question here is: Do you need friends who blame, then demand such a lie?
- ➤ Unfortunately, we live in a society that does demand such lies in order for us to be acceptable. So now the question becomes: Is being acceptable worth selling your soul?

Anger

We all want to be connected. Angry is the way we often do that when we don't know how to connect with love—usually because we don't know real love. When angry we cannot be rejected, for we have gone to that place where out of our own fear, we have rejected them first. Fear and love are both energies—fear, being an energy that is opposite of love, it cannot co-exist.

It is an either/or choice that we make—to love or to fear. In the duality of life there is a tipping point between *sweet* and *sour*, called *tasteless*. Just so, there is a tipping point between *love* and *fear* called *indifference*. Anger is a form of fear, and certainly one at the extreme end.

While this has already been alluded to in this book, at this point I will give you a necessary peek into Book Two. The following is a partial quotation from law number twenty-one concerning real love:

Real love begins with seeing your self-worth—and loving yourself. Until you have self-love, you have no real love to give to another.

——— — — — ———

See Life's Laws:
3   Thoughts are energy: loving, or not loving (fear).
4   The energy out, returns in kind.

Questions/Exercises to Consider:
- ➢ **If anger** is your choice, how much of your relationship can possible exist in the energy of love?
- ➢ **Indeed,** how much of your relationship that you perceive as love, is actually fear?
- ➢ **Or is** your "love" just a fearful need to fill an emptiness—an indifferent space—within?
- ➢ **If that** person you are angry with is your significant other, isn't it likely they are the perfect one to teach you self-love. After all, aren't they someone who sees the worth in you?

The Root Element of Wisdom

There is life, and there is death. Somewhere in between—if we are courageous enough to look at the truth of who we are being—there is wisdom. Could it be that "to look" is the root element of wisdom? For our "truth" and our "wisdom" are one and the same.

See Life's Laws:
1   I am the creator.
8   The world is not "out there"—it is "in here."

Questions/Exercises to Consider:
- **Can there** be wisdom without truth?
- **This is** your life. Do you want to know the truth of it—do you want true wisdom? Go to the *Laws of Life* in *Part One* and read the full transcript of Law 8. Now where do you need to look for truth? *Write about what you find. (You likely will find this to be an ongoing process. Leave room in your workbook and come back to it often).*
- **There is** a section following *The Laws of Truth* titled, *So What's This Writers Agenda?* In it there is a quote from Socrates. What do you think he meant? *Write about that.*

Being "Normal"

There is so much that is of absolute magnificence concerning the human race. We share in that magnificence, for it is a part of us all—of who we are.

But *"normal?"* Why would anyone consider that being *normal,* is something to be desired? Being normal is to acutely reject all that is magnificent, in favor of *fitting-in* with the socially acceptable mundane.

Doesn't this mean that being *normal,* is to be the lowest common denominator of humanity. Which too, is to say not exactly vicious, vindictive, or violent, but more importantly, it is also to say not exceptional in any positive way—and certainly, not magnificent. When does a *normal* heart ever get to soar?

See Life's Laws:
8   The world is not "out there"—it is "in here."
1   I am the creator.

Questions/Exercises to Consider:
- **Have you** notice me claiming to be "not normal?" Do you now understand why?
- **Do you** now want to be able to claim the same? *Write about it.*

Perfect Perception

If I insist on looking for imperfection, I will always find it. Wouldn't I rather look for perfection? It is also there. After all, I am the creator of my perception, and therefore, my world. Yes, I am the one who creates my world, and then attracts what comes into it. *Imperfection—perfection:* Which do you think I want to attract?

The whole universe/God will jump through your hoops to make your world exactly the way you see it. If you don't like your life, don't blame God, or other people, or even the world. Rather, look to your perceptions. It is your perception of perfection that is not perfect—which brings us full circle. Your perceptions are your life, and you are their creator!

This is the hard truth. It is not some yuppie-duppie Guru bullshit! Then again, that depends upon your "perception."

See Life's Law:
8   The world is not "out there"—it is "in here."
1   I am the creator.
2   Thoughts create

Questions/Exercise:
- **If you** are "normal," you likely had a hard time understanding this one. Did you?
- **If you** understood with perfect clarity, are you happy to be "not normal?" *Write about it.*

Count on Yourself

If you count on others, you may get short-changed. It is only when counting on yourself, that you won't—if you have integrity.

See Life's Laws:
1   I am the creator.
11   Self-esteem requires integrity.
13   Our own life is our sole possession. Just so, it is for everyone
16   We only control ourselves.

Questions/Exercise:
> **Do you** get that without integrity, you can't even count on yourself? *Yes, write about it.*

Weird

We are all unique, and still, essentially the same. From the uniqueness of our thinking springs creative growth—philosophy, art, poetry, song, dance—all which is of delight to the soul. Yet for so many "unique" is labeled "weird" and considered a source of shame. Only those with the courage to let their uniqueness be, leave a mark on this world.

See Life's Laws:
2   Thoughts create
3   Thoughts are energy: Loving, or not loving (fear).
9   Others are but a mirror for us to see ourselves.

Questions/Exercises:
- **What about** you is unique?
- **What is** just weird?
- **What will** it take for you have the courage to just let your weird hang out?

Change Your Mind—Change Your Life

Remember Law #2—Thoughts create? How it says everything begins with a thought? Here is something else it means: *You can't change anything in your life without first changing your mind.*

See Life's Law:
2   Thoughts create.

Questions/Exercises:
- **Do you** want to change your life?
- **To pound** these last two concepts on home: Can you see why nothing can be inviolable, nothing can be sacred, nothing can be untouchable about your current beliefs?
- **I'm not** looking for validation here. If you're going to work this workbook, write down your thoughts—agree or disagree, doesn't matter. If you get nothing else from this book, learn to think for yourself. Those who know how are few. Do you?—*Again, write about it.*

Fearlessness of Innocence

Little children are immortal until they discover death. With the knowledge of their mortality, they learn fear. Life becomes a thing defended as they begin the process of becoming adults. The question then is: What do adults become when they rediscover the fearlessness of their innocent child—see how it is still there inside—and use it in striding along on their pathway in life? Do they then become heroes—or something more?

--- --- --- ---

See Life's Laws:
8   The world is not "out there"—it is "in here."
3   Thoughts are energy: loving, or not loving (fear).

Questions/Exercises:
- **Ah, the** fearlessness of the immortal child—is it any different from that of the immortal soul?
- **Think about** that one. Ask yourself: Do you want to become more?
- **Are you** aware that it is only your thinking holding you back? And *THAT,* you have the power to change.
- **What would** your life be like, were you to be in touch with a little child-like fun and fearlessness? *Write about it.*

Fear

Y'know, fear can be a useful thing—it will lend flight to your feet if you have an actual tiger chomping at your actual butt.
While that may be a possibility, that sort of thing just doesn't warrant the time most folks spend living in fear and worrying—so much time, that their life then becomes a fearful place.

Funny thing is, the greatest fear of all about life—is death. When—Where—How—

And, *OH MY GOD! What then?* That, is the greatest of the unknowns. You see, the unknown is what fear is really about.

And the worry? —The worry is that we can't handle what we are going to handle.

See Life's Laws:
14   Change is the constant of the Universe.
3   Thoughts are energy: loving, or not loving (fear).
1   *I am the Creator.*

Questions/Exercises:
- **Is it** possible that worry is really the same thing as stupidity?
- **And fear?**—If you insist on teasing tigers, then you are right to fear. *List your fears.*
- **What do** you worry about? *List that also.*
- **How about** tigers? Are there any actual tigers prowling your life?

Standing by Your Beliefs

My strength in standing by my beliefs, must always be tempered by a willingness to look at what it is I believe—to recognize just what is it about me, is served by that belief.

While my belief system guides me in life, it also limits. Growth is about releasing those beliefs that don't serve me, and adopting those that do.

Sometimes our *"strength"* in holding to our beliefs can cause us to lose that which is most precious. This process is called *"foolish pride."* Foolish pride *never* serves, for it always demands your loved ones believe the same as you.

Making demands on another's beliefs, most often begs resistance—at least from anyone who sees the "fool" in foolish.

See Life's Law:
8   The world is not "out there"—it is "in here."

Questions/Exercises:
- **Ah, the** "strong mindedness" of one's forefathers: Can you see one of society's lies in there somewhere?
- **Then how** about the unshakeable belief in one's religion? Both the beliefs of our forefathers and of our religions are sacred—inviolable. Or are they? *Write about it—all of it.*

Whole and Healed

We all walk a different path in life, because we all have different needs. The parts I need to fill, or the wounds I need healed, are not the same as yours. And, we are always being offered the lessons we need to become whole and healed.

Yes, God, The Creator, the highest part of our soul, guides our personal private journey, offering the truths we need to see about ourselves—truths we don't always accept.

Those who do, are the courageous ones. *Truth*, is what it takes to become whole and healed. We don't tell ourselves lies out of love, y'know? Rather, out of fear—a fear called cowardice, It is only cowards, who won't accept the obvious truth.

Once you look at and accept these Spiritual Laws, they are nothing short of obvious.

See Life's Laws:
9   Others are but a mirror for us to see ourselves.
5   The Universe Always Balances
3   Thoughts are energy: loving, or not loving (fear).

Questions/Exercises:
- **How much** of your dysfunction—your wounding—do you think is caused by the lies almost all of us were taught, and believe to be the truth?
- **How much** do you think is because we tell ourselves lies, because we don't want to accept the truth? *Explain—give specific examples—this is NOT a math lesson on unspecified percentages.*

Standards

Everyone must have certain standards to feel okay with themselves. Sometimes these are about things they will never allow to happen in their lives—and, sometimes things they must have happening.

As for the standards of others—the yardstick for them is the same one as for you. ACTIONS! Our standards show up in the things we do, and sometimes the things we don't.

You get to create your life the way you want. After all, you are its *creator*—always. And always too, you set its *limits*. Your standards don't limit how high you fly; only how low—and, who you will fly beside

See Life's Laws:
1   I am the creator.
13   Our own life is our sole possession. Just so, it is for everyone.
8   The world is not "out there"—it is "in here."

Questions/Exercises:
- **If you** were to raise your standards for yourself, what would that look like? *Again—specific actions.*
- **As for** the standards of others—you do know that *they* don't limit to how high you fly—*YOU* do. *Who in your life have you been blaming for holding you back?*
- **Now about** those you have just listed above . . . *Sure, you care about them—AND, this is your life—your only life. You know what you must do. Will you give them the opportunity to live theirs better, by your example?*
- **By raising** your own standards, those you fly with will either be left behind, or will raise their own. You don't have the right to demand your standards be theirs. *You do know this—right?*
- *Did they stay, or were they left behind? Go to Part One and read the full text on Law 5—Write about it.*

Illusions of Security

My thought system is the box that encompasses my world, and provides an illusion of security. In truth, it is what limits my very being.

To increase the scope of our thought system is commendable, and sometimes even daring. But dealing with those illusions of security? —Now that takes real courage.

You only feel secure if you think you control everything and everyone in your world. Let's look at some who thought that—Hitler—Stalin—Mao—to name a few. How well did that work for them?

Only the courageous can accept that security does not exist!

See Life's Laws:
8   The world is not "out there"—it is "in here."
14   Change is the constant of the Universe.

Questions/Exercises to Consider:
- **This isn't** the first time this has been mentioned. Do you accept that there is NO security in life?
- **Can you** understand why these feelings of insecurity almost guarantee you will try to control those around you?
- **Do you** think the understanding of security being an illusion might be harder for a woman to accept than for a man? One of the lies they have been taught is that they need a man for protection and security. Protection, maybe—but security? *What do you think?*

Accept

Again, when I won't accept the *"What Is's"* of my world—those I have no control over—then I guarantee myself pain. When I ignore or refuse to deal with my pain accordingly, then I guarantee myself a dysfunctional life.

When we won't accept our loved ones as being who they are, then we guarantee ourselves pain. When we insist they change to suit ourselves, then we guarantee ourselves a dysfunctional relationship.

When you bounce through your dysfunctional life, always up in the air and using one or the other of these points to land, eventually you will run off your landing strip and crash. Then, the only question will be: "Will you survive?"

You may have noticed the pronoun used is *"you"* this time. This is because I once flew just such a dysfunctional life—and, I have survived. *You too*, can let go of all that painful dysfunction in your life. To change your life, just change your mind.

But loved ones? Loved ones simply need to be accepted exactly for who they are—loved ones. Especially when all they give in return, is their fear.

See Life's Laws:
2   Thoughts create.
3   Thoughts are energy: loving, or not loving (fear).

Questions/Exercises:
- **Go back** and re-read the concept titled *The Gift of Our Pain*. Do you understand that the *What Is's* (above) are actually immortal aspects—timeless? Can you see how these concepts fit together? *Write about it.*
- **Are there** things about your loved ones you don't accept? *Explain.*
- How about those things you don't accept in life—things that you cannot control? *List them.*
- **If you've** done this exercise, likely you have quite a list. If you do, ask yourself: With my thinking this foggy, will I see the end of this landing strip before I crash?

Adults Do

Adults do what adults do . . .

As small children, we often think it is all about us and interpret those events as messages. If we should find ourselves being passed around from one adult to another, and no one seems to want us, we usually decide there must be something wrong with us—that we aren't *good or worthy* enough. If we were, wouldn't we be loved, wouldn't we be wanted?

The truth is, there's nothing wrong with the child. It is simply that some adults are unwilling to love. Small children have perfect love. They are perfect. God makes them that way, every time. But who they have been taught to be, by the time they are an adult—yeah, that can be pretty fucked-up.

See Life's Laws:
3   Thoughts are energy: loving, or not loving (fear).
15   To create a functional life requires us to do our own thinking.
12   Our lives are run first by our needs—then our wants.

Questions/Exercises:
- **Were you** one of those fucked-over children?
- **Did you** become a fucked-up adult?
- **We arrive** in this world pristine and perfect—but does anyone ever stay that way?
- **Perhaps** it is simply that some of us need the experience of being fucked-over to grow and evolve. Did you? *Write down your thoughts about it all.*

Generations Past

Perception is a choice. Yet how much of your personal world is governed by the choices made by generations past?

We are born into a prison, built brick on brick by each of our ancestors—one without doors, but which to sustain life, must have a few windows. Though perhaps heavily barred, and set up high, they at least let in necessities—food, water, air . . .

I think our creator provided us each a spoon with which most, simply eat their gruel, completely unaware of their incarceration. Yet for the more awake few, we cherish that spoon, polish it, hold it up and sometimes catch a reflection of the truth through those high bars—perhaps we even use it to dig our way free.

That spoon is merely the willingness to look at one's self, while ignoring the inheritance of who our ancestors said we must be. That spoon is called honesty—self-honesty.

See Life's Laws:
8   The world is not "out there"—it is "in here."
15   To create a functional life requires us to do our own thinking.

Questions/Exercises:
- **Do you** have that kind of honesty?
- **Is there** anything about yourself that you are unwilling to look at with honesty? *If not, explain why you are the first such person in history who does not.*
- **Don't you** know that the fact you are reading this book says that you aren't just eating your gruel? *Explain how you feel about that.*

Who You Really Are

To be who you want to be, requires that you express who you really are—to take the joys that are within your soul, and express them in your life.

Your soul is beautiful and complete.

See Life's Law:
8   The world is not "out there"—it is "in here."

Questions/Exercises:
- **How do** you feel about these statements?
- **Do you** understand them?
- **Do you** believe them? *Explain.*

Our Own Reality

Everyone lives in their own reality and no one's looks the same. I must be willing to open my mind to yours, if I want to know you. Otherwise, I'll just see someone who looks like me. The funny thing is, it will be someone I won't recognize

---

See Life's Laws:
8   The world is not "out there"—it is "in here."
9   Others are but a mirror for us to see ourselves.

Questions/Exercises:
- ➢ **Given the** last concept and then this one, can you see that if you want to open your mind—see something differently—nothing can be inviolable, nothing sacred, nothing untouchable? List any beliefs you hold that you would never consider changing? *Why?*
- ➢ **What does** this say about you having a open mind?
- ➢ **Do you** understand that what you see about me, in the mirror (law 9), must *never* be ignored? *Why is that?*
- ➢ **How often** do you think that the beliefs you then see that need changing, will fit crosswise to those you listed as untouchable? Maybe—*always*? *What do you think?*

Our World

Our world *"out there"* is in black and white: Our thinking *"in here"* is what colors it.

See Life's Law:
8   The world is not "out there"—it is "in here."

Questions/Exercises:
- **Do you** color your world with the pure colors of the rainbow—the colors of love?
- **Or do** you rub that black and white into a dismal grey, or mix love's colors into an odious brown, and them flush all light with a swirl of fear, like a toilet over a black hole?
- **Two extremes**—one of love, one of fear. *Which do you choose?*

About Blame

Blame is just a lost opportunity to get honest with yourself—the lie you find easier to face than facing the truth.

See Life's Laws:
2 Thoughts create.
1 I am the creator.
7 Being the creator requires responsibility.

Questions/Exercises:
- **Can you** see that in blaming others you make them responsible—at least in your own mind?
- **In doing** that—in making them responsible for your pain—aren't you also making yourself a victim to them. And isn't that just something also in your mind?
- **Everything** begins as a thought (Law 2), remember? How does it feel to know that blaming is about being a victim—a self-made victim—one too cowardly to face the truth? *Explain.*

Being Who You Are

You have everything you can have—being who you are, right now.
To have anything more, you must become more.
To become more you must change your mind.

———— — — — ————

Life's Laws: See
1   I am the creator.
2   Thoughts create.

Questions/Exercises:
- **This is** one of several variations of this same theme?
- **But hey,** when one has several really great ways of saying the same thing—say them all. The person listening may only hear one. Did you hear more than one? Being a variation did it add something or just bore you?
- **Did you** actually go back to see what I'm talking about? If not, did you answer this last question as "bored?" This question speaks to your level of participation. *Write about that.*

Right or Wrong

There is no *"right or wrong"*—except inside someone's judgmental mind. Inside a non-judgmental mind, there is only *"loving or not loving."*

Love is not something I can demand of another—not even something I can demand of myself. It is something I must *be*—if, I would know it for myself, or from another.

In the space of love, *"right or wrong"* are meaningless.

See Life's Laws:
- 3   Thoughts are energy: loving, or not loving (fear).
- 4   The energy out, returns in kind.
- 8   The world is not "out there"—it is "in here."

Questions/Exercises:
- ➢ **Did you** get that to *be love,* you cannot *be right* and you cannot *be wrong?*
- ➢ **Just** *being love?*—Have you ever been there? *Explain.*
- ➢ **Were they** to look, for many, being right has always been more important? *Did you look—and if so, were you right or were you love?*

The Words We Use

I should do this . . . I should have done that . . .

Whenever you *"should"* on yourself, you'll always come out stinking! You see, *"should"* is another word for *"feces of the mind."* While it is usually that of someone else's mind—some faulty thinking of theirs that you accept as true. In this case, the thinking is your own. So now, let's take it personal—let's look at you.

Because words are thoughts expressed—

And thoughts create, remember—

Then the question is: Do you really want to spread all that "should" on yourself? Do you understand why you'll always come out stinking?

The *"stink,"* revolves around the question of integrity. *"Should"* is about not doing something you think you need to do—your *thinking* does not match your *doing*.

See Life's Laws:
11   Self-esteem requires integrity.
2   Thoughts create.

Questions/Exercises:
- **Should-ing or** shitting—is either one a healthy thing for you to do on yourself?
- **In fact,** it's an odious thing to do on anyone. Don't you see that what it is saying is: "I know better than you—I AM better than you?" *Write about it?*
- **Hell, you** must know that from the personal experience of folks who have been *should-ing* on you in your own life. How often has their shit nurtured you? *Again, write about it.*

Thoughts

I have everything I want—consciously or unconsciously—right now. To have anything different, I must think different. The stuff I have that I don't think I want—that doesn't serve me—I need to search out the unconscious reason why I truly do want it, and then change that thought.

Anything—any thought—in my world that doesn't serve me in a positive manner is always a dysfunction.

My thoughts create it all. My job is to create my life. And God? God's job is to bring to me anything that supports my world as I see it.

It's all good. Any dysfunction in my life is merely an opportunity to grow. My thinking is a work in progress. Were my world completely functional, I'd have no where to grow—Yikes! What a sad way to die.

Meanwhile, living life fully requires a certain sense of responsibility: the gut-wrenching responsibility to look at myself with honesty—to recognize and maybe even appreciate my dysfunctional thinking, *and change it.* God's job is not to correct my dysfunctions—that's mine.

See Life's Laws:
2   Thoughts create.
8   The world is not "out there"—it is "in here."
7   Being the creator requires responsibility.

Questions/Exercises:
- **Do you** have dysfunction in your world?
- **If you** said "NO," are you willing to consider that lie as the first dysfunction you want to address? *Address as necessary.*
- **As for** the rest of those in your circle of life, what dysfunctions do they have? Chances are, they validate your own. *What do you think?*
- **Are you** aware that in changing your thinking and releasing a dysfunction, it is likely you will also be releasing those now supporting that dysfunction in your life. *How does this one feel?*

Commitment

If you say you won't—You're honest.
If you say you can't—you're right.
If you say you'll try—you've just not got the courage to say you won't.
But if you say you will—*you'd better!*

Or else have arranged for someone who will—because you've gone and died.

See Life's Law:
11   Self-esteem requires integrity.

Questions/Exercises:
- **We're talking** integrity here. Few people really get it. Do you? *Explain.*
- **Do you** need to copy this and stick it on your fridge?

>>><<<

Death's Whisper

Sometimes the truth of life can only be heard in the surety of Death's whisper—a whisper spoken in the darkening of a night you expect will not again lighten. Death's visit always brings death. Yet for a lucky few, it is only the death of a life of lies—and when comes the light, with it comes the gift of the truth in life.

See Life's Law:
1   I am the creator.

Questions/Exercises:
- **Does it** need to go this far before you will give yourself this gift? Or do you not see the gift?
- **Are you** afraid to look at the truth of your life?
- **I have** no room to rub your nose in this one. Death is how far it had to go before I would look at my truth. Will it be the same for you?
- **Can you** count on Death's reprieve?
- **I mentioned** earlier, this book offers you a reprieve. Do you see it yet? *Explain.*

A Weapon of Fear

When I can accept every person—weaknesses and all—only then, can I truly appreciate the person that I am. Those "weaknesses" are merely the dysfunctions once conjured by my own soul to create the pain for change.

Evolution? Change? Is it not the same? Another person's weaknesses, when viewed in ridicule, blinds you to the judgmental person you now are. Yet if viewed in love, it can only point to who you once were, and to the magnificence of who you've become.

It's about law number three: *Our choice of energies is only love or fear.* Ridicule is but a weapon of fear wielded by you—you who don't have the courage to look at who you are.

See Life's Laws:
3   Thoughts are energy: loving, or not loving (fear).
9   Others are but a mirror for us to see ourselves.

Questions/Exercises:
- **It is** the recurring theme of this book, so again, I'll ask this question: Do you have the courage to look at who you are? If so, who is it you see? If no, why not?
- **Do you** look at and judge the weaknesses of others?
- **Do you** realize that you would not even have the ability to see those weaknesses if they are not now—or were not in the past—also within you? *Write down your thoughts.*

There in Balance

The greatest gifts life gives us are nearly always the most painful. When you are finished with choosing the pain, then look for the joy in the lesson. It is there in balance.

See Life's Laws:
5   For every sorrowful thing, there exists the potential for equal joy. The Universe always balances.
10   The purpose of life is for those lessons.

Questions/Exercises:
- **Have you** ever had something almost unbearably painful happen to you, then later realized something really joyful came out of that experience? *Explain.*
- **There is** no doubt you have known such pain—everyone has. Question is: If you haven't yet, are you willing to seek out the joy? *What is your first step?*
- **If your** pain revolves around a loved one's death, do you think that person would want you to remember them with pain or with joy? *Explain*

Its Lies

You may change jobs, move to the far reaches of your universe, but you can never make your life work better—not until you recognize its lies. When your life stands on the foundation of a lie, it cannot be joyful, or functional.

See Life's Laws:
8	The world is not "out there"—it is "in here."

Questions/Exercises:
- **Have you** ever uprooted your whole life looking to make it better somewhere else? *I did—four times. Where and when did you?*
- **What, if** anything, has changed that might cause you to stay and root out the lies next time?
- **The fact** that you are reading this book says you are searching for the truth. What specific truths have you discovered within these pages that you have or will, apply to your life? *Write*

About Liars

There's just two types of liars. There's those who would look you in the eye and lie, all the while knowing it—and intending it. And then there is the rest of humanity, we who think we are honest.

I doubt there is one person alive who has not wanted to be accepted by someone he or she cared about. Cared so much so, that they put on a pretense of being who they thought that person wanted.

And then carried that pretense so far, that they themselves forgot it was a lie. Maybe for some, it no longer was—if that was who they, themselves, wanted to be.

But for me, there was a time when facing death, I realized there were too many lies. So many that I no longer knew the truth about who I was. But there was one truth I could not deny, I did not like or respect this liar I found myself to be.

That's called awakening, folks. It is the first step to true honesty.'

———— — — — ————

See Life's Laws:
11 Self-esteem requires integrity.
8   The world is not "out there"—it is "in here."

Questions/Exercises:
- **Have you** ever been there—have you taken that first step? *Write about it.*
- **Will it** take facing death for you to awaken?
  Looking at your life from the perspective of the Laws of Truth could be your awakening—if you are willing. Are you?

Endless Possibilities

The possibilities of life are endless—endless joy, or endless pain. The determining factor is: do you choose to keep your power of choice, or do you throw it away with blame?

Your choice is to live joyfully in the energy of love, or in painful blame, using the energy of fear.

When I blamed, I told the world that it was that other person's fault. How many folks could see the truth? I don't know.

Few ever called me on it. But you gotta know that few were fooled. They saw me for the liar I was. So did I—and so did my soul.

So it was, I believe, that my soul sent the Angel—nothing like a little death to make a person see the truth of his or her life.

See Life's Laws:
3   Thoughts are energy: loving, or not loving (fear).
7   Being the creator requires responsibility.

Questions/Exercises:
- **Do you** think that lying to your soul might be cause for it to hit the re-set button?

The Works of Others

Some folks manage to get quite far by claiming the good works of others as their own. In the halls of government, this is called "politics."

Those works may benefit the world, but just who are the givers, and who are the takers? Our soul is not fooled, but often our conscious mind is. It all depends on how conscious our conscious mind is of our soul.

Assuredly, a person's own gift to the world may lie in having the ability to take the ideas and expertise of others, and organize it all into something of great value.

There is no shame in leadership. Leaders give credit gratefully, knowing that without the good works of others, they have nothing—they are nothing. This is the mark of a true leader.

It is only in your good works, wherein there is true joy and nurturing for your own soul, and in turn, the world.

See Life's Laws:
3   Thoughts are energy: loving, or not loving (fear).
2   Thoughts create.
4   The energy out, returns in kind.

Questions/Exercises:
- **What are** your own good works? *List them.*
- **If you** can't, then you need to know that no one is worthless.
- **Do you** think it's time to get to work looking within and discovering the worth in you? *Will you?*
- **Do you** know your contribution to this world is in sharing what is inside you? *Again, will you look?*

No One's World is the Same

We all live in a world of our own, comprised of every belief we hold as true. No one's world is exactly the same—the Spiritual Law, remember?

And yes. I know, I've been beating this one black and blue. But if you're still conscious, read on—

Thing is, it is where our world intersects with another's that we find a certain exquisite joy—a special oneness. Feel free to rub up against everyone you meet. Your life will be made richer. Because if you choose to look, you can always find some truth in their world that will expand your own.

———— — — ————

See Life's Law:
8   The world is not "out there"—it is "in here."

Questions/Exercises:
- **Whose life** have you rubbed up against lately?
- **Did you** find something that enlightened your own life?
- **If you** got slapped, then you've gotta know: There's a difference between one's life and one's body. You do know that, don't you?

Taking Offense

Whenever I'm busy "taking" offense, I am giving absolutely nothing to anyone—except maybe to myself, and that would only be a bad day.

And if you're going to have a bad day, make sure the "offense" is one of physical personal security.

Emotional offenses are only taken by the emotionally insecure—the flaming victims of the world. For them, offense is the spark they strike that ignites their fearful insecurities.

See Life's Laws:
1   I am the creator.
7   Being the creator requires responsibility.
3   Thoughts are energy: loving, or not loving (fear).

Questions/Exercises:
- **Do you** take offense often? *How often and why?*
- **You do** know that it is the most cherished way that those who consider themselves victims have, for keeping themselves that way? Don't you? *Write down your thoughts.*

Selfish Wants

Your wants *of* another are most often selfish. Your wants *for* another are most often loving. The trick is to be honest enough to know the difference—and, to know when to keep your wants to yourself.

How often will a want be fulfilled when it is a demand? Demands are only made *of* another, never *for* another. A want *of* another, is the one most often voiced, and also, most often denied.

See Life's Laws:
13   Our own life is our sole possession. Just so, it is for everyone.
16   We only control ourselves.

Questions/Exercises:
- **So, what** the fuck **DO** you want?
- **Do you** want it "of" someone, or "for" someone?
- **Or did** you get all hung-up taking offense with the word "fuck?" If so, here is another law to consider: *If it is in your face, it is a lesson, a test, or a validation.*
- **This lesson** was just given in the last concept. So it must be a test, because it damned sure doesn't validate that you got that last concept. What do you think?
- **"Cheap shot?"**—Yes! But only for those flaming victims who would see it that way. *Do you?*
- **Following the** Laws of Truth, as presented here, will make you the master of your life. Don't see it? *Tell me why not.*
- **This whole** book is about me offering you the understanding of this one basic concept: *You are either a victim in your life, or the master of your life. Which do you choose?*

Conventional Thinking

If you are busy blaming others for how you feel, you are also busy trying to control them by holding them hostage to your feelings.

It is the "conventional" way of thinking. Do you wonder why there is so much sickness of the mind and dysfunction in our society? Could it be, it begins with you?

See Life's Laws:

7 Being the creator requires responsibility.
8 The world is not "out there"—it is "in here."
13 Our own life is our sole possession. Just so, it is for everyone.

Questions/Exercises:
- **Did you** take offense with this concept, or of the two prior—many will? If so, can you see the advantage of thinking a little more unconventionally? *Discuss it with yourself.*
- **If you** are NOT into blame, and control, and taking offense—hell, you must be just as bat-shit crazy as I. Give yourself a pat on the back—*and then write about it.*
- **In this** book are things of which many will take offense. Consider: what if that were my gift to you to see the truth of the "who" you now are—something that cannot be seen by a conventional mind? *List any truth you didn't see before, but now do because of this book.*

Wants and Demands

Your wants speak only of yourself. Be wise enough NOT to make them *demands* of anyone, except yourself.

See Life's Laws:
13   Our own life is our sole possession. Just so, it is for everyone.
16   We only control ourselves.

Questions/Exercises:
- **Do you** want to add this one to your fridge door too?

>>><<<

Maturity

Maturity is simply becoming secure about who you are.

The mark of a secure person is that they don't require you to change anything about you. They are okay enough about themselves that nothing else in the world need change, for validation.

---- -- -- ----

See Life's Laws:
13   Our own life is our sole possession. Just so, it is for everyone.
16   We only control ourselves.
8   The world is not "out there"—it is "in here."

Questions/Exercises:
- **Do you** ever feel the need to change other people? *C'mon. Everyone's done that.*
- **Have you** ever asked someone to agree with something you knew to be bull-shit just for the validation? *And that too. Write about it.*

Ticklish

Why is one person ticklish when another is not? Could it be that ticklish for them is simply about having a body that is set on an automatic "don't touch me mode?" That consciously or unconsciously, the mind does not want the pain it has experienced, from contact with others in the past.

Then again, it could simply be the teaching of love—from loving parents tickling the laughter from their children.

Pleasure or pain—It can be so confusing when mixed on such a cellular body level.

In what other ways have you experienced pleasure being mixed with pain? Have you ever been spanked, and then told it was because they loved you?

Whoa! Have you ever been spanked while making love?

See Life's Law:
15   To create a functional life requires us to do our own thinking.

Questions/Exercises:
- **Do you** think that ticklish is just a physical thing?
- **Or is** it more in line with something called body or cellular memory?
- **If you** can think of other reasons for being ticklish, *list them.*
- **In the** future when you reach out and touch someone, if tickling is optional—will you only do it in the energy of love? *(This is not about being kinky).*

The Blind Spot

Remember how Law 9 states that others are but a mirror by which we can see ourselves—that what we don't like in them is only the thing in us that we don't want to admit is there.

It's kinda like my motorcycle mirror when I'm riding. There is always a huge blind spot dependant upon how solid my butt is planted in the saddle. The only way I can see into that spot is to get real squirrelly in that saddle—to make a deliberate effort to squirm my butt cheeks around and look.

If I don't, it's just a matter of time before that spot becomes deadly in my life. Mirrors are made for looking back and seeing things—mostly things about you. Don't you think it is time your butt cheeks got to squirming around instead of staying planted so solidly in the saddle of your ego?

See Life's Laws:
9   Others are but a mirror for us to see ourselves.
10   The purpose of life is for those lessons.

Questions/Exercises:
- **While working** this book, have your butt cheeks been squirrelly?
- **If not**—well, y'gotta know: It's no fun to get run over by the semi of life. Maybe you might consider turning that ride around, and cruising down this road again. *What do you think?*

Participation

These reflections are provided for your consideration, written as a personal gift—me to you. But a gift to really *be* a gift, requires someone to accept it. So let's talk about how this book has been accepted in your life.

That you are still reading it this far in tells me you appreciate it on some level. Is it because it has helped you in learning the lessons of your life? Or is it just part of your search for knowledge. If so, then it is not about the lessons —rather it is an excuse to avoid the "doing" part of learning those lessons?

Life *is*, about those lessons, y'know. So let's look at your life, and just how "alive" you are living.

Your willingness to go beyond those questions that only require a "yes" or "no" answer speaks loads about your conscious participation in life. You may want to pay close attention to the questions and/or exercise part of this reflection.

——— — — ———

See life's Laws:
10   The purpose of life is for those lessons.
11   Self-esteem requires integrity.
1   I am the creator.

Questions/Exercises:
- **In the** "questions" section, do you have an opinion or experience about a particular reflection that you could express, but won't, preferring to answer with a "yes" or "no"?
- **If your** "yes" or "no" answer was not the truth, do you know you are avoiding the question?
- **If it** was the truth, then doesn't you lack of explanation say you are avoiding the answer?
- **Is your** life one of what is least expected, or is it one of participation?
- **Did you** buy this book for "knowledge," or to help you change your life?
- **Does this** reflection have your hemorrhoids in a pucker?—*You may want to go back through this workbook and do the work you avoided doing.*

To Be Cherished

Sometimes in life you get to touch a stranger in such a loving way that it makes a difference to their entire life—giving them something they could never have had without you. Sometimes they honor you for it in their heart. That is the highest award you can receive: to be cherished in someone else's heart forever—someone you did not know, and may never see again.

There was once a woman who gifted me with a ticket to a seminar here in Las Vegas. While I don't know her name, and have not seen her since, she is cherished in my heart—forever.

See Life's Laws:
4   The energy out, returns in kind.
6   The energy of thoughts must flow.

Questions/Exercises:
- **Have you** done something for a stranger just out of the love in your heart?
- **Do you** think they cherish you for it?
- **Did you** have any expectations of them?
- **Does it** make a difference that you had nothing to gain other than giving someone your love? *Explain all of the above.*

Being Authentic

Worrying about how others see you will prevent you from being authentic—*EVERY TIME.*

See Life's Law:
13   Our own life is our sole possession. Just so, it is for everyone.

Questions/Exercises:
- **Are you** one of those who worries? Why is that?
- **Do you** know that what others think is personal—and none of your business?
- **Will you** stop worrying?—The key word here is "will." It is not "can."
- **Isn't all** that pink paint getting expensive? Write about what the cost is to you.

The Last Haunt

I have known the boney embrace of the Angel of Death, and had so much then that haunted me. And since, under that piercing stare, have come to witness the true magnificence of life.

And now . . .

A few remembrances—a few sweet songs—and let the ashes fall to the winds and the canyons of Southeastern Utah, my final homeland. However that last goodbye goes, the best I can wish for is that someone remembers some spark of my life I might have shared, and kindles it anew in their own—and then passes it on.

Ah, to raise the energy of the world just a little—for the single question that haunts me now in considering my going is: *Did I give as much as I took?*

Perhaps this book will kindle a spark for you—perhaps you, will do the giving for me.

See Life's Laws:
3   Thoughts are energy: loving, or not loving (fear).
6   The energy of thoughts must flow.

Questions/Exercises:
- **Do you** think it has kindled a spark—or will? And of what would that be?
- **Have** *you* given as much in this life as you've taken? Will this book help in that endeavor?
- **Death** *will* come for you and you don't know when. Did this book give you answers about your life now—answers you will want to know then?

Epilogue

As the title suggests:
Don't paint your turds pink—don't put the lie to the truth that has nurtured the "who" you are. Most have been slopping that pink paint around so long, that if they ever did know the truth, it has been forgotten. My hope is that you've used this book to search out the "who" you are beneath that paint. You will find there is nothing you'll want to cover—and no stink to embarrass you. There's only beauty—such beauty as would rival the most exotic of butterflies.

THAT . . . is who you are! That is who we all are. My most endearing wish, is that we would all choose to look for, and find that beauty—even if but for a brief glimpse. That glimpse will transform your life. If through my own stumbling redneck efforts in writing this book, you may catch that glimpse—hell, my life might then have made a difference. And so I say this final thing one more time—but differently. If you haven't yet, I hope you now will hear it.

As the spiritual law states: **Thoughts create.** The truth of who you see yourself to be, IS who you are being. Are you a crawling larva, or are you that butterfly. Your soul is that butterfly—and more. In this life your thinking is what limits you. You are here to grow your thinking.

In the end, The Angel of Death comes for us all. Question is: Will you be the butterfly?

The Assessment

Go back through your workbook and reassess those things you marked with a circle of resistance. If you find you no longer feel that resistance, then *put a checkmark next to it.*

These workbooks are not about being *right* or *wrong*. This book is *only* about seeing the workings of *The Laws of Truth* in your life. It does not have to be the same for *you* as it is for me. The point of this book is to give you some real truth —*the Laws*— and then **to get you to look within yourself**.

This assessment is to tell you if it did that, and if there has been any change in your thinking. If there has, then this book has been instrumental in changing your life.

Change your mind, change your life.

And, there is one further thing this book is meant to show you about yourself. Go back through it and note whether you still have any circles of resistance with resentment not yet checked off.

(OX!)

If there are, then I would coach you to get, and do *Book Two*. There is another assessment in the back of that book.

AGAIN, do NOT cheat yourself by reading that assessment before you have also done the work in that book.

REDNECK SPIRITUALITY

Book Two

If Shit's In Your Face...

Something's

Stinkin' In Your Thinkin'

One Last Thing

There is a concept titled "Participation" near the end of this book wherein you were asked to take note of those in the question sections that could be answered with a simple *yes* or *no* and to look at your level of participation—did your participation end with a yes or no answer? Book Two is the next level in your participation. It is NOT by way of a sales pitch that I say this. This is currently a two-book series. Book two is more advanced in its concepts, covering much that book one does not. To give you a small taste, there are an additional ten laws, one of which is as follows:

Law 26—Change requires truth.

You cannot change anything about your thinking unless it is the truth about what your heart wants. And you cannot change anything about your life without first changing your thinking. Change your mind, change your life. (Yeah, it is a law). Pretending to accept someone else's thinking, is to live a pretend life—never sustainable, always dysfunctional.

* * *

If on one of those *yes* or *no* questions you realized that you had something dysfunctional going but you simply didn't care enough to change it—fine. You cannot make changes your heart doesn't want.

Simple—yes! And, you may want to go back over those *yes* and *no* answers and consider the ramifications of your lack of participation. Are you cheating yourself out of realizing the consequences of that dysfunction—by not becoming fully aware?

A Redneck Example:

What if you have always farted whenever you felt the urge. Barring wet surprises, that has always been functional for you. But hey, when you fart in public, that energy may not feel loving or functional to others—especially in places like elevators.

Others in that elevator are going to find you extremely unacceptable and consequently will stay away—just as soon as the door opens on the next floor. *Now* you realize why you have so few friends. *Now* you see the dysfunction and have a reason to care enough to want to change. *Now* you can and will change.

That change is now sustainable because you are making it for you—

As a Final Exercise:

> Go back over **every** question that pointed out a dysfunction about you, or your thinking—those that you did not think warranted further thought or action. Consider what the true consequences may be to your life. Use the blank left side pages in your notebook to write about what you now see.

This might be your most difficult exercise. It requires brutal honesty and is meant to give you an indication of what stinks in the elevator of your life.

About the Author

Generally the author has someone else write this section—some do, and some only pretend to. But this book is about the truth. Here's a run-down of the crude realities of my redneck life.

Yes, the picture is of me—a redneck, long haired, bearded, tattooed, big biker dude. Why would someone like me be writing a book about spirituality? I've never been considered an intellectual, much less a "spiritual" one. And this subject is one that doesn't interest that many men—at least not in my circle of life. Nor did it interest me back then—but that was before. . . .

Meeting the Angel of Death was an experience that shook everything I thought was true about life—and few with such an experience will ever get to share it with you.

Who am I? Let's start with who I am not. I'm not rich or famous—never accomplished anything that set myself off as "special." And I'm certainly not a "religious" man. So it is certain that I have no need to preach anything to you. Preaching carries the expectation—if not the demand—that you believe.

I make no such demands, nor do I give a rats ass if you believe. But one thing I KNOW is that if we don't share ourselves with others, we make no difference in this world. Again, back to the main issue—who am I that I have anything to share with you?

I'm just a man who has experienced the truth at the end of his life, and knows what is important and what is not. Someone who now sees all the dysfunctional lies that once ran his life—lies you may also want to see. Our parents, our societies, our religions---all share much the same lies, and unknowingly passed them down through the generations, to us.

And that, YOU have the power to stop.

Born in Utah and raised by good Mormon parents, theirs was a religion I just never swallowed. All that my ancestors loved and held so dear, I did not. So I choked and faked my way through life, pretending to be that "good Mormon son." But what did I feel?—guilt mostly, and a growing disrespect for who I was pretending to be.

Perhaps I took after my birth mother. She too, was sort of a black sheep to the faith. A "good time girl," she bounced through two failed marriages. Having lost custody, she stole me from her in-laws and escaped to San Francisco, where with my half brother, Mark, it seemed we just got in the way of her "good times."

So it was we found ourselves in the Sunnyhills Orphanage near San Anselmo, California, where we survived for the next year. I was four, and Mark was seven, when distant relatives showed up to adopt.

Me? I was just happy to have a mommy again—Mark, was not. The child of his soul was so deeply wounded that he hid it away under a cloak of invulnerability—a cloak called "dare devil." The only thing that ever pierced that cloak was death. In December 1964, at the age of twenty, he was killed in a shoot-out with police.

I never had the kind of meanness that allowed him to shoot that cop, nor was I much of a dare-devil. Mark's courage was focused on facing death, but I accepted the rejection that drove his demise. Any courage I had was focused on facing life.

After a year at the University of Utah, my education was cut short by the draft. The year was 1966 and all my fellow soldiers were being sent to Vietnam. I was not. It seems my parents had applied for, and received, a sole survivor status for me. I was sent to Korea where I met, then later returned and married a Korean woman.

We had one son. Being a responsible redneck, I went to work turning wrenches for the next thirty years. And the new pretense—the lie now was in pretending to be the husband my wife demanded, a pretense that slipped about once a month. She'd threaten divorce, I'd beg and plead—whatever it took—then hand my balls over for the next months squeezing.

This was where my life was when in 1992, while ski-tubing in Lake Powell, I took a flip and pulled something in my lower leg. A silly, almost nothing little injury, it almost proved fatal. A week later found me in a hospital. A blood clot had broken loose from that leg and was lodged in my lungs.

The doctor ordered me to stay in bed, with my legs never over the edge—not for any reason. Then to pray that the meds would dissolve that clot before any more broke loose—and that the "clot buster" meds wouldn't kill me first. As for using the facility—Elvis may have made it famous, but for me, I shuddered at the thought of being found dead-on-the-pot. Still, when the choice was between the bedpan and dead-on-the-pot, I took my chances with the pot.

Even so, death was very real, and very present. For those ten days—real or imagined—I was face-to-face with the Grim Reaper. And the Angel of Death was not someone to whom I could tell lies.

With all pretense stripped away, and at the age of forty-five, I found myself asking who I really was, and what my life had been all about. One thing was clear: this life was all I'd ever had, and it looked to be over without my having lived it.

All those years pretending to be someone else—living a lie—were years not living. That was the life others demanded of me—but it was never my life.

So between myself and that all-too-real presence I'd come to call "The Angel," I made a promise to seek out the truth of life—if given the time—and to make mine, a life that mattered.

That was nearly twenty-five years ago. Since then, I've been searching for that truth. I've looked in various metaphysical and spiritual groups, read volumes of self-help, spiritual, history, even religious books. And I've done experiential self-help seminars, both as a participant, and later on endlessly more, support teams.

At the same time I was supporting those personal growth seminars, I became a Personal Life Coach, having graduated from Coach University in 1998. Now I write books about it.

Through it all I found that the truth resides in the Spiritual Laws of Life. In applying those laws on my journey, life became functional. Living by their truths has given me a perspective others seldom get to see—a perspective I have offered within this book to those of you who are aware of your journey, and who perhaps, are looking for direction.

Yes, the journey is one within. Some go—and some would rather die than face their own truth. Most won't look until they meet face-to-face with the Angel—and it is a sure-thing they will some day. It is not a sure thing that they will get a reprieve, like me.

NOTES

NOTES

NOTES

NOTES

NOTES

NOTES

www.ingramcontent.com/pod-product-compliance
Lightning Source LLC
Chambersburg PA
CBHW020417080526
44584CB00014B/1365